HOW TO LOVE

Arthur A. Rouner, Jr.

Contemporary Discussion Series

BAKER BOOK HOUSE
Grand Rapids, Michigan

ISBN: 0-8010-7622-6
Copyright 1974 by Baker Book House Company

Printed in the United States of America

Second Printing August 1975

Contents

Preface

In the days when marriage was new and beautiful there never was a young husband who did not intend to love his wife. Isn't that what it's all about?

But loving your wife isn't that easy these days. Loving anybody isn't that easy—your wife, your husband, your brother, your sister, your parents, your kids, your neighbor, and, certainly, your enemy!

We live in the era of "doing your own thing," of the liberation of the individual to do what he wants to do regardless of anybody else—even to those other anybodies to whom you may owe something. Plainly and simply, it's a selfish world. And selfishness itself has been given a place of honor and privilege philosophically and socially that it has not had in many generations.

So loving someone, giving yourself, and pouring yourself out—for someone else, anyone else—is something not many are urging us to do or showing us how.

This little book does not presume to have all the answers. But out of an attempt over the years to help a lot of people love each other, it does dare to offer a few of the answers—quite possibly the best ones.

An eager company of people who really wanted to know those answers, who came week by week to hear them, had much to do with stimulating and encouraging the writing of this book. My own children, who delighted in contributing suggestions of whom to love, kept me going further than I'd planned. My wife, who makes it easy to love her, has been much of the inspiration. And my secretary, skilled typist and willing friend, sufficiently believed in the cause to get it legibly on paper for me.

It was fun to produce it. I dearly hope life may be more fun for those who read it.

Arthur A. Rouner, Jr.
Edina, Minnesota

1

When Love Is Gone

(An Introduction)

It's a matter of love. Marriage is a matter of love. Family life is a matter of love.

I've listened to hundreds of husbands and wives talk about each other. I've listened to scores of kids talk about their parents. And I'm convinced it's a matter of love. As sure as I'm alive, I am convinced that the problems of family life and marriage in America are problems from the lack of love.

It's not a matter of too much money or too little money. It's not that life is moving too fast or that technology has taken over or that people aren't educated enough or that poverty and prejudice deprive people of a chance.

The problem is: "I don't know how to love him!" For all the love-talk in America, for all the love-stories, for all the images of being sexy and beautiful or handsome and athletic to be loved, and for all the novels, movies, and advertisements connecting everything in our society with love—*we don't know how to love*. And because we don't know how, we often simply do not love each other!

So many of the popular songs are about marriages breaking up, about divorce, about fathers loving their little boys but not their wives, or about young husbands leaving home "on a jet plane."

I've sat with many men—good, honest, upright, respected business, and professional men—who have said of their wives, "I just don't love her." Or, just as often, "I don't feel anything for her." And I've listened to wives say the same about their husbands. I've sat with couples when one has looked across the room right into the eyes of his or her partner and said, "I do not love you anymore."

My work as a suburban minister has taken me even into divorce courts, more times than I like to think, as a witness to the failure of love in these couples' lives. "Would you say there is no love left between this husband and wife?" the court has asked. And I have had to say, "No. No love. No love left."

And that tears me apart. Nothing has hurt me more profoundly and personally as a minister nor hung as a darker pall over my pastoral life as the firsthand witnessing from my ringside seat of the overwhelming tragedies occurring before my eyes in the lives of people who are dear to me as friends and, indeed, as Christian brothers and sisters. And I was so apparently helpless to stem the tide of grief and hurt being inflicted on each by the other.

A New York writer and public relations executive, using the pen name of Albert Martin, laid bare from his suburban home in Stamford, Connecticut, the sense of stark tragedy that was overwhelming him as he became, in 1973, one of 1,848,000 Americans who were divorced in that year. He writes,

> I don't want to be, but I am horrified by the prospect. I think it is the most devastating thing that could happen to my family, but it is going to take place.
> My wife wants it.

We would seem to have everything to live together for. We have four wonderful sons who need us both; they range in age from 6 to 16. . . .

I thought we were a perfectly happy family until my wife told me, without any advance warning, that she didn't love me anymore and wanted a divorce. Not a matter of infidelity or alcoholism or beating or arguments or desertion, but that it didn't mean anything to her anymore and she wanted out.

I have been waking about five o'clock each morning for the last year, hoping that this nightmare had gone away. I have wept more than I ever thought I could, hoped, prayed, but the reality remains, and it won't change. It seems to me impossible that so much happiness and so much sadness could be happening in the same lifetime. But we go grinding slowly, torturously, and inevitably toward a divorce.

Then he described poignantly that new sense felt in our time of people being free to just walk away from relationships to which they had long since committed themselves.

. . . We are now in a time that says that you get in touch with yourself, find out what your needs are and then fill them. That is paramount.

My wife accepts that completely. She needs freedom, independence, out from under what she felt was a smothering relationship; her whole outlook on life has changed. I don't fit into it any longer: so, divorce.

I don't feel that way, but I am left with a crumbled view of a marital world that doesn't have much popularity anymore. I feel that relationships aren't disposable; that you just don't throw them away after more than two decades. That married life is a whole spectrum . . . and of recognizing—above

9

all—that everyone has problems, and that you work at them together for the happiness of all. . . .

I ask myself: at some point, doesn't a counter-revolution have to take place? Don't the excesses in favor of the liberation of the individual have to be met by a consideration of the needs of families, of the other party? Doesn't a psychology that hands a license to a wife to do what she wants in these times fueled by the themes of Women's Lib have to be called to some accounting of responsibility?

Doesn't someone in the new psychological movement have to come forward and say: "My God, wait a minute, what are we doing to ourselves?"[1]

Love—such a hard thing in life. Such a hard thing to do well, to do responsibly, and to do selflessly and supportively. We blow it so easily. All kinds of love relationships we blow badly. And we don't know how to recover. We don't know how to make it right, to restore relationships, and to get onto the right track again.

One of "the flock" once accused me of having preached for a year and a half on love. "Isn't it time," he said, "for another theme?" But, I think, "Why be disturbed by this emphasis on love!" I stand everyday amid the shambles of the broken love of people precious to me—and I'm supposed to get off the subject of love! When have we needed more to love and to be loved—to talk about it, to think about it, and to learn about it—than right now?

Of course, *love* is a very vague word. It seems so general and without definition and, at the same

[1]*Minneapolis Tribune*, Sunday, July 8, 1973, p.13A

time, so personal and emotional. But it is a word, a quality, and a reality of frightening power. And if we do not somehow learn to understand it, use it, and grow with it, all our relationships are in peril. What do you do, for instance, if a man is your father and you do not love him? What do you do if there's a woman you live with, eat dinner with, go to bed with, take vacations with, and share children with—but do not love? What do you do when love is gone?

If we're confused and hurt and honestly want an answer, there really is one—as long as we're not put off by where it is found. Many people want answers, but some answers they won't accept. As a book of good counsel about love, the Bible still ranks as the best thing we've got. And the Bible says we should go to the source, to where love comes from. Go to that one in human history who said: "I have loved you, even as the Father has loved Me. Live with My love. When you obey Me you are living within My love, just as I obey My Father and live within His love."

You know who said this. It's Jesus. And the reason He said that was "so that you will be filled with [His] joy. Yes, your cup of joy will overflow!" He wants you joyful, glad, happy in your love, and not miserable, angry, and full of hurt. After all, husbands and wives get married to "make music together" and to be happy. Children come into families for laughter, love, and new life!

The audacious suggestion in the Bible is that there is a Someone who can find your lost love. He can give it back, recreate it, put it on a whole new footing, and give you a new chance at love. There is a Someone who can draw your family close again;

who can give your life together purpose, power, laughter, and life again—through His own gift of love.

No matter how we may want to deny it or get out of it or soft-pedal it, *love is the only way*. Jesus said, "I demand that you love one another as much as I love you." He knew that He and His friends would never make it in all that was ahead unless they loved each other. The world would be too much. The mission would be too much, the task too traumatic, and the deed too demanding without Jesus' own kind of love burning and shining as an eternal flame at the heart of their common life.

We moderns, on the other hand, have fallen into a view of love that's different from Jesus' view. We've sold ourselves the idea that love is pure emotion or all feeling; that if you don't have butterflies in your tummy every time you look at your wife, or your husband, you don't really love her, or him; that it's all over—the relationship's no good anymore and you'd better quit.

A young man, approaching forty at the time, with three fine children and a beautiful wife, told me once that he was moving out. He couldn't stay home any longer. He was sorry, but he had to go.

Why? Was he having an affair? Was she? Was there some deep, hidden problem? He said, "No. We argue. She's been sick, has a lot of pain, and isn't much fun anymore. We both have short tempers. But mostly, I just don't love her anymore."

So what? Who ever said you were always going to love your wife? You promised her a lot more than that you'd love her! But the amusing thing was that he was a highly intellectual guy who had always characterized himself as highly rational—a head man, not a heart man. But here he was giving the whole game away to the heart! He had promised a girl that he would live with her, support her, and stand by her until he died—even if she was sick and even if they did argue. Even if they came not to like each other very much!

You might have thought that this man of reason would say, "Well, a promise is a promise. I may feel one thing but I will do what is right, which is my bounden duty. We've made a family. We have these kids. They all need me as much as they need their mom. I am their father. I do have an obligation—so there's nothing for it but sticking it out and making it work." But instead he said, "I don't love her, so why should I stay?"

It's a "new morality" that says that. It's Erich Segal of *Love Story* and Margaret Mead of modern anthropology and a few other popular philosophers of American life who say, "Marriage should only be temporary. Fifty years is too long to expect any two people to live together. Two-and-a-half years is about as long as most marriages retain their vitality—five years at the outside!"

And the kids have found that idea very attractive—that we shouldn't have to be legally or morally bound forever to another person. It ought to be free and easy! Live it up as long as it's fun, positive, and not too much of a hassle. But if it gets heavy, man, when it becomes a downer—then split, man! As one of my young drug-addicted friends used to say, "I don't like being obligated to anyone. It's being obligated that puts the pressure on. I can't live under the hassle."

And I sympathize. Life is a "hassle." But when you're a top college graduate, a reputable vice president of a top financial organization, and a self-styled rational man who is supposedly influenced by logic—then you're responsible enough to know that life is a hassle. After all, in your whole business and professional dealings you live by obligations. And you honor them. Indeed, you would soon be out of business if you did not honor them.

All this could be said, perhaps, to be the "old morality." But in the Scriptures Jesus suggests that it is the eternal morality. He insists that love is deeper than feeling.

"How do I love thee? Let me count the ways . . ." (Elizabeth Barrett Browning). Love is a promise. Love is standing by. Love is not giving up. Love is forgiving your husband or your wife. Love is mucking through, making the best of it, or "hanging by your thumbs" as Bob and Ray used to say.

After all, if you have children there's no other way but to love them. There is nothing else you can give them that is any substitute for loving them. They need you in the morning and they need you in the evening. And they need both of you!

I know how easy it is to say, "Well, the kids will survive. They bounce easy. They understand more than we think. They'll be okay no matter what happens to us!" I've said that. I used to think it. But children don't bounce easy. They break.

They may in the end survive. But there is a price. And they do pay. And we as parents—ready to go our separate ways—are so cruel in how much we make them pay.

What Jesus wants us to hear loud and clear, and what He wants us to see straight on and unequivocally, is that there's just no other way than love. It's our duty before Him. "I demand," He said, "that you love each other as much as I love you."

"And here is how to measure it," He says. "The greatest love is shown when a person lays down his life for his friends. . . ." Therefore real love is measured by sacrifice.

This is very different from good feelings. And very different from tremors in the tummy. And very different from endless good times and from sexual fun and games. The test of love is suffering, enduring difficulty, putting up with problems, and letting someone else's life be more important than your own.

This is the uniquely Christian character of love. This is the Jesus-touch that makes love as we know it different from the understanding of love in any of the other great religions or philosophies of the world. With all the interest among collegians in Herman Hesse's *Sadartha*, the widespread vogue of eastern religions, and the fascination with meditation and the occult, it is tempting to idealize the Eastern, meditative, soul-cultivating traditions as just the ticket for times like these. With all the pressures of Western society, what better escape could there be than the yoga thing with its physical and spiritual introspection, quietness, and contemplation?

But bedazzled youth miss the fact that this Eastern thing is almost completely self-concern, a looking within. It's motivated by a desire to subdue the physical elements of life, to retreat from the stark realities of human existence, and ultimately to achieve a state of nothingness, of "Nirvana"— which is literally "far out," "out-of-sight!" It's out of the sight of the world, and it's out of sight from the problems of people—from the darkness of their despair and from the struggle of their souls to survive.

What Jesus says, however, is that love lives in the world where there is pain, where darkness is every day, where Pulitzer Prize-winning poets jump off bridges, where middle-aged men lose their jobs, where the teen-age children of leading citizens become addicted to drugs, where suburban mothers quietly become alcoholics in their loneliness, where professional men and civic leaders fall into love affairs and lose their perspective, and where many broken hearts go silently weeping through life unheeded and unhealed.

Jesus' love says you don't turn your back on that. You don't cultivate just your own little soul. You sacrifice. You serve. You suffer if you have to. You endure. You bear the burden in the heat of the day. You put up with people. You "weep with those who weep . . . you rejoice with those who rejoice." You take people where they are. You listen to their heart, you hear their cry, and you share their pain. You suffer with them, you get under the load, and you walk in their shoes. You say, "I'm here, with you. Don't be afraid." You share the spirit of Jesus and say, "Come to me all of you who work hard and are burdened and I will give you rest" and "Wear my yoke—it's easy and light" and "Look, I'm always with you—right to the end."

You say it even to your wife. Even to your children. Maybe even to your parents. You say, "Look, I'm with you. I'm right there physically if I can, but I'm surely with you in my heart, in my caring."

This means, frankly, putting up with the whole thing, with some of the garbage of life and with all the awful strains of growing and of changing. This includes the moods, the seething angers, the horrible arguments in the middle of the night, sleeping on the couch at times, the storming out into the night to drive madly down the highway wishing you could die, the three-day "mads," and the household wars between the generations. This includes all that mess that makes you sick—the mess that you never bargained for even if you did say, "For better, for worse, for richer, for poorer, in sickness and in health—till death us do part!"

It's the "Whither thou goest I will go" spirit of Ruth, which some would call bondage. There you are, chained together—the marriage marathon. But Jesus calls it love, real love. The measure is giving up your life for the one you love, which is exactly what He did for those He loved. He gave His life on the cross. "No man takes My life from Me," He said, "I give it up of My own free will." I know couples who have stood by each other through emotional illness and alcohol and through the years and the tears. And they're still together. They're beautiful. They've learned something.

Love means more than not having to say you're sorry. Love means forgiving after being hurt yourself. It means giving up things you care a lot about, even giving up your life. It's because you love.

We don't see much of that, although it's there in our world. Mother Theresa of Calcutta is one of the most beautiful modern-day examples. And her young "Sisters of Charity" share her self-sacrificing commitment to the poor and dying of the world. She said,

> These girls wanted to give their best because in our society we have to make a total

17

surrender to God; this is the spirit of the community. They wanted to achieve this fulfillment in their own lives by giving all to God, giving up their position, their home, their future and dedicating all of it wholly to the poorest of the poor.

Real love is measured by sacrifice.

This may sound impossible. To a lot of us it would seem beyond us. A cute young matron once talked with me about her searching for something to hang onto in her life, some way to find comfort, encouragement, and hope. "I came looking for it in your church over a year ago," she confessed. "But I was going through a divorce, and you were preaching on love and marriage. So I haven't been back."

I thought, "Here, I am, trying to help some hang onto a marriage; it must sound pretty self-righteous and judging to the poor divorced people. Their marriage has been blown already. It's too late to do anything about it. And now they're looking for help just to survive. And maybe to build a new life and find a new love."

And I'm for that. I've married plenty of divorced people. I've even married some people twice—to two different partners. So I know divorce happens. And it hurts when it does. But it does happen. And there is no guy or gal in my congregation I condemn because he is divorced or even because he is having an affair, or because he is on drugs or on alcohol, or in jail, or anything else. I answer midnight calls from bad people as well as good people. My dearest friends are people who are sinners —big sinners. Some of them are people whose lives are so mixed up that you wouldn't believe it. Three-cornered affairs right within the flock! In spite of that, I try to help them in any way I can.

18

My job isn't to judge. "Judgment is mine," said the Lord. He'll do that for all of us soon enough. I'll be judged right along with them. And I am reasonably certain that I will not stand any better than they on the Judgment Day. I'll be counting on mercy as much as they.

As a minister and friend, I've got to love. The greatest tragedy of all of life is not being loved and not having anyone care. Mother Theresa says,

> I have come . . . to realize that it is being unwanted that is the worst disease that any human being can ever experience. . . . For all kinds of diseases there are medicines and cures, but for being unwanted, except where there are willing hands to serve and . . . a loving heart to love, I don't think this terrible disease can ever be cured.

The real hope for us all is being loved by Jesus. It's being His friends. "You are My friends if you obey Me." This suggests that the way to find love is through obedience. When love is gone, only obedience ever finds it again. And that means real obedience to Christ.

Jesus was really saying to His friends, "Love isn't automatic. And the resources of My love won't come to you for nothing. You've got to be open to Me. So, you're My friends if you obey Me. That is, if you keep open to Me, keep walking with Me, talking with Me, letting Me be part of your life. You may still be a sinner. You may blow everything. But if you believe in Me and love Me, I will show you a way. I will give you the love you seek. I will help you. I will save you—save your relationships, your marriage, and your family."

Maybe, if we're praying everyday for our teenagers or for our wives or our husbands, and we are

19

really holding them up to God, asking Him to humble us, to show us how we can change and help and be more sensitive; and if we're reading the Bible ourselves and as families together, really trying to learn from it and grow in our understanding; and, in fact, if we're even doing something as pious as going to church together and trying to do something in Christ's name to help the world—giving Christian service together and having a sense of comradeship in Jesus' cause as a family—and then if we blow it and still have no common ground and the whole thing falls apart . . . well, maybe then we'll have to do what we have to do with sorrow in our hearts.

Jesus is trying to tell us that if we're trying with all our hearts in the most obedient way we can to follow Him—no matter how lonely or hurt we may be, or no matter how hopelessly love seems to be gone from our lives—we do have a chance, and we do have a promise that in His time and in His way we will find love again.

LET'S DISCUSS

1. Do you think there come times for most of us "when love is gone"? Is it a real problem?

2. What do you think destroys love between two people? What kinds of things break down the spirit and power of love?

3. Do you think, as the free-lance writer suggested, that a counter-revolution has to take place against the excesses of "liberation"?

4. Is there a good kind and a bad kind of liberation for people bound to each other in a marriage?

5. Where is the original "source" of love for all human relationships?

6. How do you tap into that source?

7. Does the "new morality" of temporary commitments as long as there is a "good relationship" offer a hopeful alternative for the traditional, churchy bases of marriage?

8. Can sacrifice really be taken as a criterion and standard for love? Is it realistic?

9. What is unique about Jesus' concept of love?

10. Is sharing and sacrifice in marriage a source of bondage or freedom? What do you think?

2

How to Love Your Wife

Wives are really special. Think what they have to put up with. Think how many husbands have been followed about from pillar to post and from job to job by their wives, all because those gals believed, in the spirit of biblical Ruth, that it was their duty! They really believed, "Whither thou goest, dear, I will go."

Of course, in the new liberated day for women—even for wives and mothers—the duty of wives to follow husbands around is not quite so universally assumed anymore. Far from it.

But even that change has come partly from the frustration everybody seems to feel these days in loving anybody. It's so hard to love. Hard even to love your dear and dutiful wife. And she deserves love more than most.

These are days of great self-centeredness, when more and more people are bent on fulfilling themselves. They do what they want to do—without regard for others. "If people stand in your way, mow 'em down!" That's the spirit of it. So if you're "fulfilling" yourself and letting your ego ride high, it's pretty easy to forget how to love another. Even your wife.

Well—how do you love her? A man could get in a heap of trouble by telling other men how to love their wives. One of the early lessons I learned as minister of a country parish was that there are some things people—at least New England Yankees —think are too private to be anybody else's business. A wild tale about the minister who had preceded me revolved about his almost being run out of town because one Sunday he presumed to tell the flock how they should organize their sexual lives. "Don't tell us, you little pipsqueak, how often we're to do sex with our wives and husbands. Bug off! Talk to us about something you know something about!"

So married love and life is at best something very difficult to talk about. It's a private world and a very possessive world. It's a place where the tampering of outsiders is not welcome.

I learned that all over again one afternoon in our city while I was out on my hospital rounds. As I was leaving after a visit, I walked through the hospital lobby on my way to my car and saw a group of girls crowding in with a couple of young men in the midst. One of them appeared to be playfully pushing one of the girls. He was a husky chap, well dressed, coat and tie and the works. As I drew near, however, I realized that several of the other girls were protesting. It dawned on me then that the young man was punching one of the girls, hard.

Suddenly, to my later dismay, I had jumped in without even thinking about what I was doing. There I was, Mr. Morality, grabbing the unknown young man by the shoulder and saying, "Hey! You can't do that!"

"Oh, can't I?" he retorted, "Who are you?" I suppose I drew myself up to the full height of my clerical dignity, gave him all my titles, and probably assured him again that he wasn't to go around punching defenseless girls while I was around. As if I were the last remaining survivor of the age of chivalry—a refugee from the Knights of the Round Table! He, however, was not impressed. "I can do anything I want with this gal, buddy," he sneered, "she's my wife."

I was foolish enough to insist that he couldn't push her around no matter what she was to him. By then, some of the other girls were whispering things to me, like, "It's all right, Mister. Don't bug him. He's a Viet Nam veteran, and he can get awful angry." My guess was that he was in a lot better shape than I was, and when he challenged me to fight, I knew very well I did not want to fight. But somehow, after all was said and done, the girl retreated and I retreated, and I did not end up as a patient at that hospital myself. But it did remind me again of the private, and sometimes brutal, world of husbands and wives.

Obviously I would not like anyone to punch me in the nose. There isn't anyone who is going to let me run his marriage for him anyway. And I am only too keenly aware of what a poor example of husbandly attention and helpfulness I am. Dare I put it in print that my wife mows the grass, rakes the leaves, and shovels the walk (some of the time), and changes the fuses (all of the time). And there are very few repairs she can get her husband to do—in spite of his insistence that, as an old Eagle Scout, he has his "handiwork" merit badge. She, in fact, has her own brand of woman's liberation. And there I stand in all my fumble-footed, mechanically-minimal glory.

Nor am I among the A-1 representatives of those who spend leisurely evenings at home with the wife and find extra time with the kids.

In the wife-loving department, I am a struggler and a straggler with all the rest. And yet I write about how to love each other because of the tragedy in marriage and family life I see all around me. I still think we all need to help each other as much as we can. I am also hopeful we might let the Bible help us and even let the apostle Paul, who seemed to have so much trouble with women, help us.

One of the things Paul said was, "Honor Christ by submitting to each other." And we want to say, "Do you mean I have to do that to love my wife?" We all know there is something in us that doesn't want to "submit," that resists giving in or conceding anything to anybody. "I'm not going to give in!" our ego demands through our gritting teeth. We'd rather go right to the brink of disaster than to submit our will to that of another human being.

And that—plain and simply—is sin. It's vain, arrogant, human pride. Something within us demands to be always right, and that part of us is so hard, so unbending, and so unloving. And *loving is caring about the other person.* Loving is being sensitive to where he or she is. It's being more interested in how the other one feels than in how we feel; more interested in what the other one needs than in what we need.

And probably the toughest thing in human relationships for any of us is breaking the pattern of pride. What Paul gives us, first off, is motivation—a reason for putting ourselves down for the sake of someone else. And that motivation is a man. And that man is Jesus. Jesus' life is a motivation. He broke the pattern of pride in His own life. He put Himself down and gave Himself up for us.

"I died for you, My children," the hymn sings, "and will ye treat Me so?" Our cruelties to each other, our proud put-downs of our husbands and wives, are really put-downs of Christ. "Inasmuch as ye have done it unto one of the least of these my brothers or my sisters, ye have done it unto Me." "Unto *Me*," He said.

Those of us who claim at least to be Christians really kill Christ with what we do to each other. Our infidelities, our angers, and our retaliations toward our wives and husbands drive nails through the hands and heart of Christ just as surely as the nails driven by Rome's legionnaires two millennia ago.

But the apostle says, "Honor Christ by submitting to each other." Care a little bit about each other by honoring Christ. Don't do it for each other if you're so mad and hostile. Do it for Jesus, whom supposedly you love. In fact, do it for the One who is love—the One who alone in all the world can give you back your love for each other and who can change your mood from resentment to tenderness. Have a care for each other, then, for Christ's sake.

Remember how angry and hurt the young couple were in the film "Love Story"? When they finally came back to each other that tough, tragic Italian-American girl philosophized, "Love means you don't have to say you're sorry."

Which seems, in a lot of ways, like bad advice. We *do* need to say we're sorry. For the truest and deepest love really knows we are sorry when we hurt each other. Shared love knows that the other one is sorry even as he or she does the cruel things.

Love's big task in loving a wife or husband is literally putting yourself under the other person, making it your mission to be under him or her. This means to listen, to learn from, to be sensitive to, and to have a heart toward him or her. And that task does give a special honor to Christ. After all, that is His way, His style, His method, and His power. Both have to give in!

Now this word for the girls. Take a lead from your husbands. Give him a chance. Offer him a little dignity. Give him a place of honor at home!

"What?" you say: "Whose side are you on, anyway? You male chauvinist pig in sheep's clothing—how dare you tell us to knuckle under to these ego-centered males at home! What century are you in? Haven't you heard we're liberated?"

I know you'd hit me if you could, but let Paul in the Scriptures say something here. "You wives," he says, "must submit to your husband's leadership in the same way you submit to the Lord."

That old apostle may be a lot wiser and more sensitive and understanding than we usually give him credit for. "In the same way you submit to the Lord." Now that's asking for a different kind of submission than most gals think they are being asked to give their husbands. We don't harbor a big resentment for the Lord, do we? We don't mind trying to love, honor, and obey Christ. We may not succeed, but we don't resent the process of trying. He, after all, deserves it. And we know that He loves us. We're sure about Him. We know He cares about us and is reaching out to us in tenderness, gentleness, and compassion. We have no doubt about His motives. We trust Him. He's proven His love for us. What more can you do to prove yourself than to die for somebody?

That's one reason why I often ask young couples

preparing for marriage what they care most about in all the world. What, for instance, would they die for? And none of the young men, oddly enough, has ever suggested that the one thing he would be willing to die for is the young girl so soon to be his wife!

If we're willing to submit to Christ without question because we trust Him and are sure of His love, then maybe we've got to get our marriages on a basis that will have the same kind of trust. Shouldn't anybody who's going to marry another person commit his life and his future to that other person in trust? You surely don't marry someone you think is going to do you in! Why is humbling our proud egos to that one other human being who means the most to us in life, so hard?

Of course not all of us husbandly types are worthy of that kind of trust. But I think we could be. I know some men who are all of that right now. Their lives are fine, quiet, and devoted. And they are loved, honored, and I'll bet, in a beautiful and balanced way, obeyed. They are obeyed in the sense of being respected, honored, and admired. And this is in no way demeaning to their wives. I would guess that it's in a way that builds up their lives together into a beautiful, sharing partnership. Really, it's the very thing a lot of liberated women would love to have their marriages to be.

Do you know any men, for instance, whose wives are sick or battling some dark and difficult disease, but are men who nevertheless carry on honorably, self-sacrificially, and uncomplainingly? They go to work every day, doing their job, and then come home to be nurse, cook, comforter, and companion. They remain on duty all through the night, haunted, maybe, by what could be ahead with life so constricted and limited. They give up a social life and hardly have a sexual life. They do things they never even knew anything about before. Yet they're smiling, still giving courage, and doing what they have to do. They keep the flags flying, keeping honor bright, keeping the heart right, and looking always toward the horizon and the light. Those men are heroes in my book. They are Christians of the most courageous kind. They are men of honor and beauty and Christlike caring who shame the rest of us.

It's possible that they didn't become that way just by themselves. Maybe it didn't come easily. Maybe they became worthy of their wives' honor, and respect, and admiration, and even "submission" because their wives in the first place gave them something that they had not deserved at the beginning.

Maybe those gals loved and honored them in such a way that chivalry, service, and gentle affection were the only things their husbands could give in return. Love, after all, begets love. Love given creates love in the person to whom it is given. Perhaps Paul the apostle understood this. Maybe he somehow knew that if a wife treats her husband like a king that he'll be a king, and he will treat her, in return, like a queen.

Aren't a lot of men in the suburban world really treated at home as something less than at least they could be? Aren't some of them viewed at home as an Archie Bunker? They're not taken very seriously. They're treated as sort of an incompetent. Maybe some guys really are out there working their hearts out for their families. They really want to be something more to those at home. Wanting to be credited with having some wisdom and ideas worth listening to isn't that bad. Maybe there doesn't always need to be a challenge, an argument, or grief. Maybe if the girl of his dreams listened lovingly and respectfully to him, he would learn to live lovingly, respectfully, encouragingly, and companionably toward her.

Could that be the message?

But that's not all. There's this word for husbands. Love your wife sacrificially. "And you husbands," Paul says, "show the same kind of love to your wives as Christ showed to the church when He died for her . . . that is how husbands should treat their wives, loving them as part of themselves."

The whole responsibility can't be put off on the gals. A wife can help a man to love her, but the burden isn't hers to start the process. The loving business is a willingness to work against your own self-interest, to live for someone else, and to give all for the love of another.

And most of us love ourselves too much to do that very well. As Paul suggests, we do a pretty good job of taking care of ourselves. Can you imagine loving your wife as much as you love your own body? Can you imagine cherishing her life as much as your life? Maybe our wives feel too often that we husbands would make any sacrifice asked of us for the company, the job, and do it immediately with no questions asked. And they may feel that making a sacrifice for her or the kids is secondary to our work.

Not that we don't have our job to do or that our families don't want us to do it. But they'd like to feel that in our hearts they count just as much as the job. They need to feel that they are loved, too: that we still enjoy them, still love being with them, and still are enchanted, excited, and made happy by their company.

It was a sobering moment in my own life, but a beautiful one, to read a note my wife had left on the seat of my car at work on a day when there hadn't been much said as I left in the morning. It was at the end of a week when we felt we had hardly seen each other. "One of the many good moments of my life," she had written, "was Tuesday evening to hear you say, 'I'll call Mrs. _____ later, my son needs me now.' " It could be my sons, my daughters, or most of all, my wife. Time just with them doesn't happen often enough.

There's a tragedy in our busy, important lives. And it is that something's lost from the romance of those courting days. Most of us weren't into the work thing in the same way in those days, and our hearts fluttered and flip-flopped when we saw that beautiful thing who's now our wife.

You know, she's still beautiful. She's a lot more mature than she was then. She understands us better. We've shared life together. We've been through a few things together. Why can't we be lovers all over again? Why can't we nurture and care for our wives in the way Jesus nurtures, leads, shelters, heals, forgives, and up-builds His church everyday? Maybe we could say we're sorry. Maybe we could surprise her with the little attention—the unexpected word of kindness and the small act of tenderness.

I, for one, think we don't hold hands enough. We don't look each other in the eye enough, or laugh enough, or tell jokes enough, or be silly enough, or take picnics enough, or hold each other enough, or pray together, enough. And praying together in a marriage is something for the guys to do as a start in leading the way. Take her hand and say, "Pray with me, honey."

It at least could be a start. It might make things a lot better this year. It might make life and love and marriage better for always.

Love those gals, Christian men, the way they deserve to be loved and the way you promised to love. It's the way the Lord loves us and wants us, now, to love.

LET'S DISCUSS

1. What do you think are the special needs wives have to be loved?

2. Do you think there really is a philosophy of putting yourself first—of "doing your own thing"—that keeps people from loving others?

3. Why is marriage so often a possessive relationship? Should it be?

4. Is "submission" to a wife or husband any easier if we think of it as submission to Christ?

5. What primarily keeps us from submission to another human being?

6. Do you think that saying "I'm sorry" helps? That praying helps? Have you tried?

7. Can wives help husbands be their best? How?

8. Do you think most husbands could be taken more seriously than they are?

9. Do you think a husband "doing himself in" for his wife would make a difference in their relationship?

10. Can wives really become as important as their husbands' jobs? Any reason why they can't?

3

How to Love Your Husband

In some suburban marriages the husband is viewed as the bad guy. Not only do some sociologists say so and some wives think so, but, some husbands themselves believe it.

Many husbands have a deep sense of guilt—an undercover, undefined, and almost fatalistic feeling of failure in their role as husbands and fathers. There is a demon of defeat who berates us regularly with lectures that moralize along lines such as: "You slob, Arthur, when do you ever take time for your wife and kids? What do you really care about them? You live as though you love only yourself!"

And there is so much truth in it. The husbands, after all, are the ones with the big egos. They're the ones yearning for success. Their souls are fired with ambition. They're the ones who want to be on top. They'll go anywhere, move to any city or town in the world, and force on their families any sacrifice to serve that relentless, bewitching drive of theirs. Chained to it, they are. They become slaves of its mastery and possessed by its witchery.

And the wives and kids? How do they rate by comparison? No way are they a match. Loved deeply and dearly as most of them are, they still have not a chance. They really don't compare. When it's them against the job they always lose.

So how, for heaven's sake—and for love's sake—do you deal with such a strange animal as a husband? How do you cope with him, keep up with him, manage him, live with him, or last of all, *love* him?

Would you believe the Bible says something about that? It states some pretty good things actually, that should be of some help. Particularly good is the apostle Peter's advice in his first letter to his Christian friends.

First, Peter says something not many will want to hear, particularly the wives: *"fit in!"* "Accommodate." "Go along!" Isn't that awful? No self-respecting woman's libber wants to hear that! " 'Go along' with that guy? 'Fit in' with all his schemes and plans for getting ahead and becoming Mister Top-of-the-Pile success sensation? You've gotta be kidding! I'd rather die! What about *my* life! My ego! My ambitions? Not a chance."

Well, listen for a minute: "Wives," Peter says, "fit in with your husband's plans. . . ." And then he gives this intriguing reason, "For then, if they refuse to listen when you talk to them about the Lord, they will be won by your respectful, pure behavior. Your Godly lives will speak to them better than any words."

Some interesting assumptions are here: first, that the little woman is a Christian; that the wives are believers; and that they love Jesus. Not only that they are the ones in the marriage who are born more instinctively spiritual, but also that they have already made the specific, personal commitment of their life to Jesus. Therefore with them Jesus takes first place.

There's a little bit of woman's lib right there,

albeit a rather more exalted kind than the self-centered variety that is all to glibly accepted by many of our gals these days. It does put those men in their place, which is as men before God and equal with women. For the gals here would be giving their ultimate allegiance and loyalty not to themselves but to God—to whom it rightly belongs.

So, the gals are not caught in a personal two-way contest with their husbands. They're no longer out to put him down, or out-point him, or show him up. They're already seeing him in a different way—as a child of God, as somebody Jesus loves, as somebody Jesus is interested in, and therefore as somebody *they* can be interested in. The husband is somebody who, after all, has needs. He's a person. A person is somebody to be loved and maybe even sheltered and shielded and affectionately supported just the way kids are assumed to be unquestionably protected and upheld and defended and loved. A husband is not somebody, then, who has to be viewed always as the friendly enemy.

So, the wife doesn't always have to head him off at the pass. He just may have some good ideas about something besides his business. Quite possibly going along with even his bad ideas isn't always the worst plan. Most of us, after all, need to be trusted and to be honored and thought well of, sometime, by somebody. And even if your man is admired by all sorts of people out there in the big world, including various adoring secretaries and other women—maybe there's only one person in all that world whose admiration and affection and respect he really craves and cares about. Yours.

And look at something else: Peter in the Bible is also assuming that your husband isn't a Christian. That he isn't quite there yet. That he's not as pious as you are and hasn't gone as far in spiritual things, perhaps, as you have. That he's the big man of the world who has to listen to the rational, hard-nosed, down-to-earth ideas of businessmen or engineers or lawyers or scientists or what-have-you—and gets pretty well indoctrinated with that stuff. You could say he's well-nigh inoculated against faith, tenderness, spiritual sensitivity, and that whole unseen world of God's ultimate and deepest truth.

So let's say you're looking for a way to get through to him for Jesus. You don't want to browbeat him, push him, or crush his ego. You want him to buy Jesus because he wants Him. You want him to love Jesus for who Jesus is and also for who he himself is and for what he knows his own need to be.

And you'll never get him by saying, "Let's go to church, dearie — hint, hint!" But Peter says that if you "fit in with your husband's plans" and are prepared to lose a battle in order to win the war, you may be way ahead of the game. Your very wise concession, which is kindness and love, will get you further with your friend.

That's why a minister-friend of mine, who's made a specialty of counseling and giving talks to groups of couples about marriage, always asks the wives, "You know what husbands need most if they're going to go along with you? They need B-U-T-T-E-R, butter!" Don't kid yourselves, gals, there's truth in that.

What the Bible is saying to us is: "Try it." You may be surprised.

Peter also says, "Try being beautiful inside." This in no way is to discourage outward beauty. It's a sad day when either gals or guys in marriage allow themselves to get out of shape. It's sad when you get the vibrations from a marriage that the wife is expressing perhaps all unconsciously, "Well, I've got him so I don't have to be beautiful anymore." Maybe she's gained ten pounds with every baby, and she justifies being not slender and not beautiful and not healthy or vibrant physically with the rationale, "Well, I work hard enough at it without having to be beautiful in the bargain. I climb stairs all day and do errands and wash and iron clothes and operate a taxi service for kids and cook meals. So don't tell me I ought to exercise or eat less or be something I'm not. Any husband better jolly well be satisfied that he gets that!"

Of course, husbands let themselves sag on the same grounds. "Look . . . I go to the office everyday. I'm making a lot more money than you ever thought I would, dear. After all, I provide pretty well, wouldn't you say? I don't have time to exercise. I have to do a lot of my business over lunches and dinners, and I like cigars. So if I look like an overweight, middle-aged, cigar-chewing businessman, it's because I am. I have to be. Don't ask me to be a Steve McQueen or a Robert Redford!"

But the Bible says, "The body is the temple of the Spirit." This puts a pretty high priority on the physical and on health and beauty. There is no reason, from the biblical record, to think that Jesus Himself was anything but a beautiful man. It says in fact that He "grew in wisdom and stature, and in favor with God and man!"

So beauty's all right. God doesn't knock that. But He does say to the wives, through Peter, "Don't be concerned about outward beauty that depends on jewelry or beautiful clothes or hair arrangement. Be beautiful inside, in your hearts, with the lasting charm of a gentle and quiet spirit which is so precious to God."

And it's precious to *men*! The inner spirit, the beauty inside, the instincts of love and caring —these qualities of the heart—are a high priority with men. In fact, it is interesting that the women married men fall in love with in affairs are often not nearly as physically beautiful as their own wives. They're seeking something else. Something inside. They're looking for someone who will love them, support them, and yes, even admire them!

Aren't there a lot of wives who, while they expect their husbands to say "I love you" to them and expect to be admired and told they are beautiful, assume either that their husbands have no interest in being complimented and verbally supported themselves, or assume that somehow it just goes without saying? In other words they assume that their husbands already know that they are admired and really don't need to be told.

This is a grave mistake, friends. Would you believe there are many men who feel that somehow they are not greatly admired by their wives? At least not in the enchanting, exciting, and "mean it" way they'd like to be admired and cared about. Many men feel very much taken for granted, and, in fact, not really taken seriously at home.

Outer beauty is nothing without the inner fire. The gal who laughs, smiles, has fun, is interested in her partner, is obviously thinking of him, is concentrating on him, and is loving him, has something to offer that a gorgeous model with a heart of stone can't begin to compete with. The expressive, loving heart will always beat out the beautiful body that is only a body.

Love poetry. Be interested in little things. Love people. Enjoy God's world and your husband's world. Hold his hand sometimes and be his supporter, his confidante, his friend, and you'll go a long way, baby! Try hard to be beautiful inside.

And last of all, but far from least, try making your home a place of sympathy and love. If you want to love your husband in a creative, up-building, and supportive way, make your family fun. Don't, for heaven's sake, be a fish wife—yelling at the kids, given to intemperate displays of anger at their kidly ineptitudes. Who wants to come home to a three-ring circus or to a melee of competing forces all fighting with each other?

This doesn't mean it's all your responsibility, girls, to be a lion-tamer with the task of keeping the cats in their cages. Husbands are fathers, too. And they also have a job at home. They have a huge influence in the home, and they've got to exercise it.

Every institution has a certain style and spirit. Every government administration, every business, every faculty, and every family. People in families have a way of doing things, of relating to each other, and of communicating. And maybe the most profound way in which that communicating process of talking, sharing, and thinking with each other is affected all day long is by the mood of the mother. It doesn't mean a husband and father can't ruin it all if he comes home so tired and hurt by the knocks he's taken in the business and professional world that day that he jumps on everybody. The author offers that as a personal confession.

But, how nice and what a relief when kids can just laugh it off and say, "Okay, everybody, cool it—Dad's had a hard day!" It's great when kids can have a sense of humor and not take their father too seriously that day and can just humor him along until he falls in line and can laugh, too—even at himself. That's love at work. And you know whose love? It's mom's. It's the wife and mother who has set the mood, who has been loving and caring and helping the kids be that way, too.

Wouldn't you suppose that on any given night your husband could go either way? He could get ticked off and be angry, or he could enter in, be supportive, and so be a beautiful addition to the family circle—the friend whose presence is eagerly welcomed.

It's pretty standard for lots of mothers to consider it their moral, bounden duty to be at home when their kids return from school. They wouldn't think of not being there. One mother I know still makes tea every afternoon and invites the kids to sit down and just talk about their day and what's been big in it for them.

Husbands may not be kids, but they are in their own way little boys, and they like to be welcomed home, too. Maybe it's not spoiling them or giving them a false honor to expect them home and to greet them with love, warmth, and joy. Maybe he's been knocking himself out in the cold, cruel world for you. Maybe he's even failed. He may not even be bringing much in—but he loves you and, whether he says it or not, he's doing what he's doing for you.

So love him. Get out of the jeans and get gussied up—just a little—for him. He needs that. He loves you. And even if he hasn't been very nice the last few days, and even if you don't think he loves you as he should, he'll do a lot better if you'll love him. It's pretty hard to be a rat when your wife throws her arms around your neck and kisses you and says, "Love you, dear," "I've missed you, dear," "Glad you're home, friend." He may respond in surprising ways. In fact, he may be so surprised that he'll be a whole new guy that night and nice to everybody. He'll be so glad and so grateful for you and the kids.

In the Bible, Peter says, "And now this word to all of you: you should be like one big happy family, full of sympathy toward each other, loving one another with tender hearts and humble minds. Don't repay evil for evil. Don't snap back at those who say unkind things about you. Instead, pray for God's help for them, for we are to be kind to others, and God will bless us for it."

That last word could be a beautiful secret key with which to open up love with husbands and with families. "Pray for God's help for them, for we are to be kind to others, and God will bless us for it." Pray for your husbands. That's not really too much to ask, is it, if you really care? Pray God to help them. Pray God's help for you to be kind to them. And God will bless you. Oh yes, He will. He will do for you what no marriage counselor or divorce court could ever do. He will change it all around. He will bring you together. He will give you one mind and heart, one hope and joy. He'll give you back the love you once had for each other.

And it will be better than it ever was.

He'll put fun back in your life. And lots of laughs, picnics, concerts, books read, poetry shared, walks in fields, long talks, stars in the eyes—and huggin' and kissin' and prayin' and believing and hoping and living on and on till we all make it to our Fiftieth intact!

It'll be beautiful. You'll be beautiful. You and your husband, together.

LET'S DISCUSS

1. *How big a problem is ambition for husbands? Does it get in the way of a loving marriage?*

2. *How big is the problem of guilt feelings for husbands today?*

3. *Is "fitting in" with a husband's plans possible for a wife?*

4. *How should husbands be "put in their place"?*

5. *If Jesus comes before husband in a wife's eyes, is that bad?*

6. *Do husbands have to be viewed as the "friendly enemy"?*

7. *Are there ways to help a husband become a Christian?*

8. *What's wrong with a wife buttering her husband up?*

9. *What's wrong with working hard to be beautiful yourself?*

10. *What special contribution can a wife make to the style and spirit of a home?*

4

Life with a Very Difficult Man

The problems that women of the women's liberation movement are having with the men in their
lives warrants some acknowledgement on the part
of men that their peculiar bundle of drives and
needs does in fact make them quite often very
difficult people to live with. That masculinity thing
is hard to shake. And men are so physical—feeling
at an early age that they've got to grow muscles,
that they must fling themselves into some sport, or
that they have to somehow on some field of battle
prove themselves better than somebody else.

The forces that produce those psychic realities in
the souls of men are deep indeed. And it does mean
that they demand a lot from their women. I am
quite prepared to believe, for instance, that men
are never really as mature as women. Those gals
who tower over them from fifth grade to seventh
grade and are said to be more "mature," or "de-
veloped," may well stay that way all the rest of their
lives. Much of life for young men in their twenties
and thirties is a game of catch-up ball. And it may
lead them sadly, in a marriage fifteen years old, to
turn on the gal who earlier worked at a job to "put
hubby through" school and later slaved over dish-
pan and diapers with babies coming along. In ac-

tual fact, they may attempt to turn the heroine they had depended on for so long in for a newer, younger model. Now that, at the age of thirty-five or forty, he is finally getting it together and becoming successful in his own right. Then all of a sudden to his surprise and delight he has a veritable bevy of professional and office-type females, if not others, too, who think this man in his emerging middle-age maturity and good looks is really something else!

How more intolerable can a situation be? The nerve of the guy to pull a thing like that. Who does he think he is? Well, chances are he doesn't really know yet who he is, which is why he is so difficult. But he doesn't want to be difficult and that makes him worth understanding by others who care. After all, he is one of God's children and maybe we shouldn't give up on him.

A New England woman I knew long ago and still love has written a book I want to read called *Life with a Very Difficult Man*. She is married to a minister friend of mine, and I suspect the title is autobiographical in its origins. But the book is not about her life with her husband, but rather about a gallant New England lady of an earlier century, Sarah Pierpont, and her life in mid-eighteenth-century Northampton, Massachusetts, with the famous minister, evangelist, philosopher, and writer, Jonathan Edwards.

I am intrigued by her title because I think there are many wives who could all too easily, if asked, describe their lives with their husbands as life with "a very difficult man." Most of us little boys at forty or so are stuck with those peculiar male egos the women's lib people talk about, as well as with a

44

childhood indoctrination into the competitive spirit in all things, including the horribly damaging doctrine that "little boys don't cry."

Therefore, what makes most of us difficult stems from what means most to us in life—what drives us ahead in our business or profession and even in our hobbies and the things we do just for fun—the burning desire—often unconscious and only rarely articulated—*to be best*. Better than anyone else. Not only do we want to succeed, to get there, but we want people to say, "Hey, you're great," "You're the best," "We admire you," "You're our ideal," and "May we have your autograph?"

And that doesn't make for very good husbands. It makes for even worse fathers. Too many things come first *before* the family. Too many "very important things" must be done before you can find time to go away for a rest or away for a few days with your wife or before you can spend an afternoon with your son or just sit and look right at him —without a newspaper, papers from the office, or anything else between you—and just listen and let him talk and you really hear and understand.

In Shaw's play *Misalliance*, the father of the young suitor, when asked by the father of the bride-to-be as to what his relation to his sons had been, confessed, "Oh, dear me, we were only acquaintances, I'm afraid. There was never any time. We nodded at each other. I'm afraid we don't know each other very well. And now we rather tend to avoid each other. It's a little embarrassing to meet, you know."

A father in my suburban flock wrote this anonymous response to a publicly written "Open Letter to Dads on Father's Day." He said in part to the bewildered son who had written the original letter:

> I wonder how much of my love for you has really been love for myself. I wanted you to like me. And I wanted a lot of nice things and nice times. But is that all that important? Was I really thinking of myself all the time and not realizing how selfish I was? Maybe I didn't want to admit it. This would have been a sign of weakness and I wanted to be strong in your eyes. A "good" provider and friend to you. You were my son and I was your father. That's a close relationship and I didn't want to risk losing you by showing you my weaknesses. So I hid. I hid within myself and by shutting you out, I shut myself in and never really let you get close to me. And I couldn't get close to you. I couldn't get past my own feelings of insecurity, inadequacy, uncertainty in order to help you.

It's so hard to be a father. It's hard to be a wife and mother, or a son or a daughter. It's hard to be a family, especially a Christian family.

It is interesting that Jesus Himself was someone with whom His family found living with Him to be life with a very difficult man. He grew up in a small town, but He finally went away, as a traveling teacher and preacher, on what His mother and brothers became convinced was a wild goose chase. They even went looking for Him just as many parents have gone searching through Greenwich Village or Haight-Ashbury in our time, looking for their lost teenagers. As Jesus was teaching the people who were crowding around Him, Jesus' family came to speak to Him. Because of the crowd they sent in their message that they were outside waiting for Him. His strange answer back was, "Who is My mother? Who are My brothers?"

He pointed to His disciples and said, "Look! These are My mother and My brothers." And He added significantly, "Anyone who obeys My Father in heaven is My brother, sister, and mother."

Looking at the family as we know it, let's ask Jesus' questions, "Who is My mother? Who are My brothers?" What kind of family were they, and what kinds of families are ours? Who are the fathers and mothers and brothers and sisters who make up the middle-American family as we know it? We are looking at the fractured family.

There's no question that Jesus loved His mother dearly, and He had been elder brother and even father-figure to His young brothers and sisters. But they weren't the people who were with Him now—believing in His work, supporting Him, encouraging Him, praying for Him, and helping Him. They weren't on the same wave-length with Him.

They were there to take Him away. As far as they were concerned, big brother Jesus had gone off His rocker and was a candidate for the funny farm. Their message was, "There, there now Jesus, sure You're an evangelist and a teacher. Of course, You're God's Son, just like You've been telling people. But You need to come along home now and have a nice, long rest in Nazareth. You don't have to be here in the city messing with all these people anyway."

They just didn't understand. They weren't for Him. They really were against Him. They were not "one in the Spirit" with Jesus. They were divided. They were essentially a fractured family.

And it is the desperate, fractured nature of the life of so many of our families today that has become the American family life-style. The family doesn't all come home when the day is done, to linger around the dinner table and later sit and read by hearthside until day's light fades and then retire together. Few husbands come home from the shop or office for a leisurely lunch with the wives. Many of us aren't even at home for breakfast. Not that it would do much good if we were. Growing kids are off at different times for different schools, all helter-skelter. Throw in the meetings at night and the business trips away and the evenings out for good causes and the drive toward the top for the guy and the taxi service operation for the gal. Lace it with a little alcohol, from both sides, and throw in a couple of dead-tired bodies finally alone together at last, late at night. They are too weary for meaningful conversation or enlightened reading, or even for very loving and eager sexual expression. Then add in the mobility factor of women as well as men and the additional factor that marriage is no longer really considered an off-limits sign to potential lovers. Put it all in the context of a time of hurtling change for teen-age kids as well as parents, allow for the youth revolution and for the second thoughts of the new middle-agers of the "Command Generation," and you've got the American family stuffed into an exploding pressure cooker!

The miracle is that as many families stay as families, and that as many husbands and wives are true to each other when the whole world would pull them apart. For me it's much easier to marry people than to keep them married. There seems so often not to be the time or the patience or the leisure for husbands and wives to talk things out. Nor is there the time for fathers and sons to be together and be friends.

The electric light, the telephone, the car, and the computer have made it possible for us to do a thousand more things in a day than a human being could dream of doing a hundred years ago. A man can be at twenty or thirty different places a day and can see as many different people.

And the little woman is no longer safe and sound "down on the farm." She's all over the place, wheeling and dealing in her own way with her own set of wheels to go in. And the kids, with their revolution in brain-power, morality, and human concern, are storming the barricades of the adult world. They are a television generation, a scientific revolution generation, a world-thinking, "instant replay" generation, who are comparing their parents with their television models and ideals. And the competition is tough.

Many of us weep for the tired, angry words we've said and for the hours of love and life we haven't had with the family and for the friend and father we never were.

And one day your teenager cries:

> Do you got time to listen to me?
> I just wanna say, let me be
> free:
> Is there fear in your minds,
> As you hear what I whine?
> Let me be free, and let me be me.
> You have your meetings, and
> Things you must do —
> But have you forgotten, I have some
> Things to do too?
> I've given time, but less time
> have you — when will the battle

49

finally be through?
There is no use fighting, 'cause
I've long since decided,
I've got to be free, and let me
be me!

A husband feels so helpless, looking at these dearest people in all the world, whom he loves so much, and seeing what he's done to them. He sees how he has hurt them, how he has hung them with fears and frustrations, and how he has failed to be the friend and father to them that he promised to be and still wants to be.

What can you do? How can you help? Change your life? Re-do the whole pattern? Reorient your priorities? Do your job in a whole different way? Retool the whole machine of your life and its style?

Some things must change, but not likely everything. You're not likely to change your profession or business and your whole style of operating under its demands. You're not likely to take to the woods or switch jobs. You could take more weekends, maybe, and certainly fight for more family time.

But the fact is basically that we're stuck. We're in the pressure cooker, and we're not likely to get ourselves out. Most of us really wouldn't be fulfilled if we could get out. The truth is, we like the pace. We thrill to the fast changes, the intellectual challenges, and the variety. That's why we made this society, with all its rocketing, ricocheting, future-shocking change, and staggering pace. Let's be honest. We like it. We made it.

But what about the family? Some people have tried to change the pattern and vary the life. Marriage and family counselors tell us that there are a multiplicity of new family stylers already here! There are serial marriages, more divorces and second marriages. More people are doing sex without marriage. More mothers are demanding that the State take care of their children in day-care centers so they can be free, particularly to work. There are communal marriages. Several families are living together, sharing responsibilities. There are children who have several adults with whom to relate.

But most of us are not quite ready for that. Most of us don't really want to share our wives or our husbands sexually with someone else. There is still that deep instinct as reflected in Tennyson's *King Arthur*: "To love one maiden only, cleave to her, and worship her by years of noble deeds."

Jesus suggests that "a man shall leave his father and mother, and cleave unto his wife, and they shall be one flesh." Bound forever! That's His way—the ideal He offers. And Ruth, from the Old Testament, adds, "Entreat me not to leave thee . . . [let not] ought but death part thee and me." And Browning buys it too, "Grow old along with me. The best is yet to be!"

We really want to believe that. In the beginning of our married relationships we all want to go the distance—to take on this guy or this gal for life! Even if it's fifty years. But the hard question is: how do you avoid the tears?

The plain truth is that you can't. But you can add to the good things you have. You can deepen the dimensions that are there. You can build quality even while quantity may not be possible. Times together can mean more. And relations of love can be experienced in depth with a wider group of people, who can be a steadying and stabilizing

51

group. In fact, we transient Americans need a kind of extended family much as Margaret Mead has suggested.

Curiously, this is exactly what happened to Jesus. When He was told about His mother and brothers being outside waiting for Him, His surprising but profound answer was, "Look! These here, these disciples, My friends and followers, are My mother and My brothers."

He was suggesting that "family" is more than blood. Family is the deepest kind of human relationship. And for Jesus, the deepest relationship He had in life was with His friends, His brothers and sisters in faith. "These are My mother and My brothers!" In Jesus' own life it was the church that in fact became His extended family.

Interestingly the pressures of our time have become so great on families that many of them are coming back full circle to finding the church —wherever it is real, alive, and loving—to be in quite a new way the center of their lives. They are finding the company of brothers and sisters they care most about, as well as the ones who care about them, who fulfill them, take an interest in them, and who celebrate the great moments of their lives with them.

The church has become a family—really *the* family—for me and my family. When I've needed it most and my wife and children have needed it most, it's been there, not just with program but with people. And in the case of my children it was not just other children and young people who were there, but other adults also were there to be their friends. They discovered mature men and women besides their own mother and father, and different from their mother and father, who love them and who talk with them, sometimes long into the night. Some were people they could trust and say some things to that they couldn't say to their own parents.

One incident especially expresses this wider family circle. Several families have been close to my children. The parents in those families are their friends and the children in those families are held in special affection. One June Sunday at the punch table on the front lawn after church, two daughters of mine were talking and laughing with the boys of corresponding age of one of those families. A young woman who loves them passed by, and seeing them together said, "Oh, are you cousins?" Taken by surprise, they looked at each other for a moment, and laughing, said, "Why, yeah—we are!"

So the church holds out to our fractured families the rather unique possibility of being our extended family.

This helps to make possible the *faithful family*. This is what Jesus Himself began and why the Christian brotherhood was born and where belief was nurtured and where God came close—among those who shared the faith with Him, among those who were His brothers in belief. "Anyone who obeys My Father in heaven is My brother, sister, and mother!"

Anyone who believes is a brother. In other words, faith makes the family. Faith creates the true family, the true marriage, the true partnership, and the relationship that God meant each of us to have.

Actually, Jesus' blood-family finally came

around. They finally overcame their pride, ignorance, and jealousy, and saw the light. They gave Jesus a place of love and acceptance in their hearts. His own mother was there, finally, at the foot of the cross. James, His brother, was there, finally, in the Jerusalem church as its leader.

The tragedy comes in where families, and the fathers or the mothers in those families, resist faith. They don't care. Their priorities are the values of self and the world and not Christ and His church. They are the parents who are appalled, mortified, and made uncomfortable when one of their children finds faith and "turns on" to Jesus. Some people have made their lives so shallow that the real Jesus, shouldering into their family through the heart of a teenager, actually is an offense to them. Because He asks so much and is so uncompromising, they cannot stand the change that would be required of them. This happens even though their teenager has come into a new life of love, joy, peace, and purpose, which is the gift beyond any pride for any human heart.

The truth is that the parents are judged. Their superficiality is exposed. So it is not unusual to witness the devastating spectacle that the avowed enemy of an eager young person's new faith turns out to be his own parents! They, believe it or not, become the ones who call their teenager a "religious nut." They've never laid the foundations of faith in their own home and they cannot stand, now, to have Christ come crashing into the midst of their self-gratifying lives and messing things up.

But this sometimes happens so gradually in our families that nobody notices. That's the way the devil does it. But there it is. If we could just wake up to what our values have become and see what's happened to us. Too often it takes an awful pain before we wake up—or a coffin to weep beside, a divorce court to enter, or the drug end of the county jail to visit.

It takes us so long. We are so blind, so selfish. The cause is really the little care we have for our kids. They cry out for God. They long for the arms of Jesus. But that's kid's stuff to us.

The Bible says "repent." Jesus says, "You fool! This night your soul will be required of you, and then who will have all your suburban trappings?"

If something so simple and available as the Christian church is, or could be, a true family of faith—an extended family of love—it might be worth getting with the church and letting its Lord make a difference in our homes.

So many kids out there need a home where God's Spirit is. Lots of wives need that too. Even a lot of husbands.

A youngster drew a flower on the order of service in church one Sunday and wrote underneath, "Jesus, everywhere, anytime you want Him!" On the other side was drawn a cross and a cheer for Jesus, "Yay!"

I don't think any man is so difficult that he cannot change his heart and lead his family into faith and say with his kids, "Yay, Jesus!"

LET'S DISCUSS

1. *Why do you think men are difficult to live with?*

2. *Do you agree that a man in his forties has some special problems both he and his wife need to understand?*

3. What was difficult about life with Jesus for His family?

4. What is the "exploding pressure cooker" in which the American family finds itself?

5. What is different about the role of women today that adds pressure to a marriage?

6. Is it true that we like the frantic pace at which most of us are running?

7. Is an "extended family" possible, even when our relatives are far away?

8. Have you found the church to be an extended family for you and your family? Could it be?

9. Can a "faithful family" be as important as a "blood family"? Worth a try?

10. Could you help any fathers you know lead their families into faith?

5

Sex, Babies,
and the Christian Life

In considering how we can learn to love each other—husbands loving wives, wives loving husbands, parents loving kids, and kids loving parents—it wouldn't be a bad idea to spend a chapter looking at what sex and the producing of babies and the creating of life and the bringing of families into being is all about.

These tend to be things we just do sort of by instinct. Like "doin' what comes natcherly." We fall in love, do sex, have babies, and start out to be families without ever looking very seriously at what marriage itself and sex itself and family life itself is all about—particularly from any philosophical or religious point-of-view. This chapter is an attempt in a modest way to take such a view.

There is a tender and rather philosophical scene in the movie "Kotch" where the young unwed mother, soon to have her baby, is sitting by the fireside with the old man in his little beach house. She is dressing bowling-pin dolls and thinking aloud about how she got pregnant. She mimics her school counselor, "Well! You could have protected yourself, dear!"

And then she scoffs, "As if I didn't know that! Who does she think I am, some kind of a tramp? It isn't as if I was going to go around doing it all the time with all the boys. Do you know that Stephen and I only did it three times, and I got pregnant? I know lots of girls who do it all the time and never get pregnant!"

And then she says, "I suppose I could have gotten an abortion—but I've seen too many girls messed up for life that way." That whole beautiful movie was the story of birth and death, of childhood and old age, and ultimately of the struggle of a little teenaged girl to understand the meaning of life and love and of the beauty and miracle of a little baby.

Erica and Kotch and that little baby are a reminder that we have come into a time of great confusion about sex, babies, marriage, and families. "The pill" has certainly had a hand in doing it to us. And so has the new and freer acceptance of abortion as a way of solving problems. The colleges' abdication of its parietal responsibility on many campuses has added its share to the confusion—as have easy marriage and easy divorce and society's perpetual readiness to bless almost everything and to look the other way.

I, for one, am so sad about marriage, so sick about sex, and so shocked at what we all are willing to do to little babies, born and unborn, that I want to offer a little of what I think God says to help us.

He says it in a beautiful story about a man and a woman who wanted a baby. They prayed for a baby. They didn't want birth control, or abortion, or an adoption agency, or a state-run day-care center. They wanted to be parents! They were even married—how about that! They hadn't slept together in dormitory rooms in college. They hadn't talked themselves into sexual intercourse before marriage being okay "as long as you have a 'good relationship.'" They hadn't tried to fool anybody. They just loved each other, and they loved little children.

One day their prayer was answered, and God said, "You will have a son. And he will be a special person. You are to name him John."

Isn't that really the way it is—that a baby comes from God? A child is born in faith. Parents are people who love you and who love each other. They love enough to be married, to be husband and wife. They wait for you, prepare for you, and say, "Look! Here he is! Born in nine months. Conceived after marriage. We're not ashamed. This is our beloved son in whom we are well pleased!"

Let's look at that story from Luke's Gospel and see what it says about the problem of love in relation to sex, babies, and the Christian life.

One thing it says is that sex and babies are a source of joy for us and for others. The angel's promise to Zacharias, the father, is: "You will both have great joy and gladness at his birth, and many will rejoice with you."

That's beautiful. It's so pure and right and innocent and glad. It's kind of old-fashioned—a pure, positive experience. Yes, we know that sex and childbirth and the whole business of babies has always had its problems. It never was 100 percent pure, unadulterated joy. There's always some agony, suffering, pain, and disappointment.

But babies today are viewed so widely as such an inconvenience and such a complication. By a lot of people they're called "trouble." But the angel didn't say, "You will call him Trouble." The baby was a person. "You will call him John, and he'll be a human being in the world. He's going to be somebody."

I listen to the current conversations of college and high school gals about sex and babies. It is so strange to me that these girls, who as a generation like to view themselves as such humanitarians and protestors on behalf of human values and human dignity—campaigning, as many of them have done, for black power, women's liberation, and an end to war in Viet Nam and Cambodia—should right now make something so mechanical and dispensable and disposable, such a *thing*, out of a human being who is closer and more intimately related, physically and spiritually, to them than anyone they will ever know in life.

For many of them a baby is an unplanned addendum to the big thing, the thing that is really important to them, which they've just gotta have, and which they so suavely and sophisticatedly insist to me is their right to have, which is sex. It is sexual play and intercourse. And they do not see sex as in any way bound to marriage. They say, "I've gotta be free to have sex—to really express myself and my love."

And they're having it. Some of the most innocent, unswinging little girls you can imagine, whose parents haven't the faintest notion that they're doing it, are having their sex. One young innocent said, "Well, there's no point in my parents knowing. They'd only worry, and they don't need to. My boyfriend and I aren't having intercourse. We're just going to bed together." All I could think of to say was "Lots of luck!" They may be smarter and more brilliant and more cosmopolitan in their time than we were, but they're sure not made any differently!

But what if a gal became pregnant and was going to have a baby? (And, of course, they really don't think it could ever happen.) But just suppose. . . . "Well," they answer, "I'd have an abortion," or, "maybe I'll get married and have the baby."

They dismiss it just like that, almost with a snap of the fingers. I suppose it's because babies at the beginning are so small. And they believe what they hear about no personality in the fetus until three months. It is a new life in their own bodies, yet they can think of it only as a "thing"!

Even if they get married, they haven't thought of that unborn baby as a person who might be hurt or destroyed by what they did. I'm so sad about so much of what I see of people's view of marriage and how they enter into it. The truth of human relationships and what they do to us has not changed. Nor has the fact changed that all our acts have consequences. Too often the cavalier beginnings to marriage and the affairs of sex for self's sake begin a trail of evil that inevitably surfaces and has repercusions years later. Too many times a marriage of ten or fifteen years that has broken down to scenes of anger, frustration, recrimination, illicit love affairs, hurt, and finally the legal break of divorce, was a marriage begun with an already-pregnant bride.

And what God really meant for us is joy and ecstasy in the miracle of a baby's birth. And, as God will have it, it's a miracle anywhere it takes place and whatever the circumstances of the conception. Even in the movie "Kotch," the birth scene in a gas station rest room of a little baby to an unmarried, teen-age mother is a beautiful picture of God's love and the wonder of a child, as that frightened little girl takes to her breast her new-born baby.

You can't get away from the joy! That's what sex and babies are about. That's what the miracle of life is supposed to give us—a joy for ourselves and a joy we can share with others. "You will have great joy and gladness. . . . and many will rejoice with you."

And to be really complete, to be deep and beautiful—a God-experience all the way through—it should be joy. "You will both have great joy," was the angel's word to Zacharias. "You and Elizabeth." A joy shared by the husband and the wife. It's something that brings them ultimately together with the whole world. God meant that there to be two of us for every child.

Following the birth of a little girl, a young husband and new father sent me the message, "How's that after eight years?" He wanted the world to know about it. But that, strangely enough, was nothing compared to their joy just a few months later. That little girl had become very ill and the prognosis was not good. They prayed and we prayed, and a way was found and she lives. And her young mother and father are convinced that it was the power of prayer and love. They later came, with great joy, to have their baby baptized among the people who so faithfully had prayed for them. Joy and gladness surrounded a baby's presence.

And God's purpose for each of His children, I think, is that each will be a person pure and faithful. There is a purpose for every child. I do not doubt God's destiny, plan, and purpose for every child of His born into the world of men. And when we've "gone wrong" and our lives have sheared off into unworthy things, antisocial behavior, darkness, destruction, and distortion, it is from defiance. It's from not listening to God, from failing to be in tune with Him. It is from disobedience. It is from sin. It is from being determined to run your life yourself instead of accepting God's guidance.

God's purpose and plan is that His children would be whole persons, pure and faithful in their lives. As the angel said to Zacharias about his son John, "He will be one of the Lord's great men. He must never touch wine or hard liquor. And he will be filled with the Holy Spirit even from before his birth."

Is a man hopelessly naive to dream of that for his sons and daughters? Children may be bad. They may go through agony growing up. Who, for heaven's sake, ever wants to be fifteen again? Not I! Oh, those endless arguments, those interminable discussions, and the irrationality! "You can take it as the rule of thumb," one of my doctor friends once said, "every fifteen-year-old is a psychotic!" This is not to say that lots of us much older don't continue to act like fifteen-year-olds.

But this is a measure of how broken and incomplete we are and of our failure to be on God's wave-length. It's our sin, the battle with evil going on inside us and the struggle between good and evil that is the daily warfare of our souls. But God's purpose is for our sons and daughters to be literally "the Lord's great men and women." God's purpose is that kids be "pure in heart."

And I would follow the Scripture here even to say that He wants them uncorrupted by any drug that makes them no longer their true selves. I mean that if you're talking about real life and about top values and true priorities, who needs it? There's nothing attractive about a drunk or an addict—whether it's a skid row derelict, a fashionable matron at a tail-gate party, a bleary-eyed teenager after a Friday night game, or a responsible citizen and leader of the community trying to steer his car home from a party.

I chanced once to be sitting at an evening discussion next to a man who impressed me as kind, good, and concerned. He was board chairman of one of his state's most powerful companies. He was a man in many ways above reproach. Most of the men in the room had drinks, as he did. My friend and I got talking about young people. In what I can only imagine was an unguarded moment, he pointed to his Scotch and water and, with a wry smile, said, "You know, I'm one of those who be-lieves in this kind of drug, but not the other kind." If the young people of America could have heard that!

That's not what God wants of us. He may love us and forgive us, but that's not what He wants of us. He wants great men of the Spirit. He wants pure hearts of innocence. And I believe He's working toward that even while a baby is in the womb. "He will be filled with the Holy Spirit," was God's promise of John the Baptist, "even," it says, "from before his birth."

What a profound insight into the power and miracle of life! The Spirit of God is working and stirring in a child's life even before he is born. And so are other spirits. We know now what a drug-taking mother can do to an unborn baby. We know that there are little children born into the world already helpless heroin addicts. We know that cigarette smoking by a pregnant mother affects her unborn baby. And psychologically and spiritually, we are learning that even the darkness and turmoil of a mother's heart passes a shadow across the spirit of her babe in the womb. There is a prenatal fear—sometimes of not being wanted or of apprehension about the trauma of the birth experience itself—that is a darkness that dogs the spirit of a child and young person even into his adulthood, until it can be healed and erased by love and faith and prayer.

What a fantastic thing we're tampering with when we mess around with the life process. We look at babies as things. We want our sex so badly that we'll bring to life a child whose destiny we haven't really considered or cared about. We're not even sure we will allow the child to live. An infant's heart and later hopes and future feelings we do not consider when we glibly enter into sex before marriage.

Why shouldn't every little child have a chance, just half a chance to be one of the Lord's great men—a person of purity and a child of God filled with the Holy Spirit in faith and power? Why shouldn't every child born into this world have a chance to grow up and write, as one beautiful college girl did to me, from Europe, saying:

> Now, not only do I "have faith" and call myself a Christian, but Christ . . . lives in me and I benefit from all the things Christ is and offers to man. . . .

She is a person, pure and faithful.

Then why not have this hope, too, for a child. To hope that he will be a leader of the people for God? People used to dream of their little sons becoming president. So why shouldn't Christians dream of a son or daughter not only being a joy to others and a person of faith, but also a leader of men? To be someone who would help other people find God? To be someone whose own life would be convincing proof to others of the power, beauty, joy, and love of life with Christ?

Around an intimate dinner table one evening a dear friend in the Catholic priesthood talked about how difficult recruiting young men for the priesthood had become in recent years. "If you grew up in a home or parish where especially newer younger priests were forever under fire and being criticized for their stands as Christian leaders, that doesn't exactly persuade young lads to look eagerly toward preparing for the priesthood, does it? When it comes to that," he said, "who needs it? What persuades young men to become priests," he said, "is to see a happy priest."

It isn't easy to raise up preachers and pastors or convinced and convincing lay Christians. But what's wrong with praying and hoping for it and holding it as an ideal if you're a Christian and you have a son?

Zacharias and Elizabeth were told more about their son: "He will persuade many a Jew to turn to the Lord his God. He will be a man of rugged spirit and power like Elijah, the prophet of old; and he will precede the coming of the Messiah, preparing the people for His arrival! He will teach them to love the Lord just as their ancestors did, and to live as Godly men."

And that was good news to those two parents. They didn't say, "Oh, please! Not a preacher for a son! Don't tell us after we've waited all these years that we've gotta have a Baptist for a kid . . . or a holy-roller or something. All we want is a good, red-blooded, all-around boy!"

They didn't think this way at all. They couldn't have wished for anything better. It was as good as being president in their book. John was to be a man who would help people find God! He was going to love the world and lift it a little bit. He was to be a child with both a tender heart and a burning spirit. He was to possess a love for people. This, to them, was tremendous! A dream fulfilled!

You know, that's all a part of sex, too. Babies have to grow up to be young men and women. And to be their friend and their father or mother is a very different ball game from merely satisfying yourself sexually when you're in college or high school. It's an awesome undertaking. And if you're not prepared to take on the whole thing and give it a jolly good try—then it is really immoral (which is to say unfair, cruel, and selfish) to be playing around with the other end of the life process.

Babies are meant to grow up. Babies are planned by God to be people. And God hasn't provided any other way to help them, encourage them, nurture them, and love them into maturity and faith and usefulness *than by parents!* People are needed who are willing to be parents. Parenthood is part of the privilege of marriage.

So, by all means, use "the pill." Conceive only the children you can love and take care of. But when a child is conceived, he's a gift of God, a treasure for your heart, and a little growing person who's going to love you, but also need you.

And don't kid yourself into thinking your kids can get along without you or that they don't really need a full-time father or mother in case you want to take off or ditch out. Too many feel that "the children" are no longer sufficient reason for keeping a shaky, troubled marriage going. "For the sake of your little son," a man in agony over his love for another woman was advised by his minister friend, "be faithful to your wife."

I believe that in the end it's worth it. It may be a sacrifice. You may not want the kids or the marriage or the wife or husband you've got. But you won't be sorry if you stand by and refuse to desert the little ones God has given you. That may very well be the kind of sacrifice that becomes "denying yourself" to follow Jesus. It may, in fact, be "losing your life in order to find it." You may feel you're giving up everything—that dream of a wild, wonderful love you never knew existed and that you can't possibly live without. You may feel you're giving up your one chance to break free and get out of a marriage that's been a drag for a long time. You may protest, "What right does any kid, even my own, have to hold me back from the happiness I've got a chance to have?"

But the much deeper spiritual truth is that Christ redeems. He changes things. He changes the human heart. He heals old wounds. He makes new and beautiful the hearts that are hurt and sad. You really won't lose. You will be given the strength to endure. And most surprising, you will be rewarded for your faithfulness by a new love and happiness from the place you would least expect it—from that very wife or husband you are so eager now to leave.

And look what you get as well—your son or daughter, growing up, becoming a man or woman, helping other people, becoming a useful contributor to the world, loving Jesus, and sharing Him with others. All the while you have the privilege of standing by in a ringside seat, having the joy of watching it happen—watching something good and beautiful unfold, instead of observing what could otherwise be, and so often is, the spectacle of a deepening human tragedy unfold, the responsibility for which your heart could hardly have borne.

I dream of that growth and maturity and useful service for my little guy who bears a disciple's name. And I dream of it too for the so many young people growing up in the family of faith around me. They are learning, making decisions of faith, and gradually emerging in their own way as "fishers of men." They are Christians of rugged spirit and power who already are helping others to know and love the Jesus who means so much to them.

They are young people like the college girl who wrote to me explaining why she wouldn't be able to meet me on my forthcoming "college visit" to her campus. She would be away at a Christian conference. "I'm going to be at Bethel College," she wrote, "to talk about Christ. I'm really looking forward to hearing the speeches and discussing with other kids about life with Jesus." Her P.S. was "Remember, Jesus loves you!" And, in parenthesis, she added, "And I do too!"

Sex, babies, and the Christian life is about producing people like that. I think it's the heart of the plan and the purpose of life. That's really what makes sex a joy and babies beautiful. It's beautiful to have the chance to be born and to grow up to be somebody, for Christ and for all the things that are finest and best in our human existence.

LET'S DISCUSS

1. Do you feel you were adequately taught the things of "sex, babies, and the Christian life" as a growing young person?

2. What were you not taught that you should have been taught?

3. Are you doing better with your own kids?

4. What difference does joy make in the coming of a baby?

5. Does a Christian view of sex and marriage have some bearing on your personal view of abortion?

6. What are some of the things that pregnancy before marriage can do to a relationship?

7. Do you think there is a place for moral "purity" in the teaching and later life of a young child today? Is it a worthwhile virtue?

8. Can you accept that God has a "plan" for every one of our lives?

9. Is it legitimate for Christian parents to hope and pray that their child will be a "great," good, significant person?

10. Would you say kids alone are a good reason for a husband and wife with marriage problems to do everything they can to stay together?

6

How to Love Your Kids

A phone call came from one of our town's police officers. He's my friend, a brother Christian. We occasionally get together to talk about our town —its problems and its people's needs.

This time it was a kid problem. But it also was a parent problem. On a recent weekend he'd been called by a distraught mother. Her junior high daughter had gone to the home of a friend with a "druggy" reputation and wouldn't come home. The mother called the police. My friend responded to the call, and he and the mother went to the home and got the girl. He took her to the station.

They talked. "Unmanageable child," the mom complained. "How come?" the officer asked the girl. "Well, every weekend my mother and father drink a lot," the thirteen-year-old responded. "And I'm afraid." She was also angry and resentful. She obviously had a very low view of herself. She felt that the world was against her. She was doing a lot of negative things. Since she was known to have come around to the church's junior high drop-in center, the officer approached me with the problem.

My friend, the policeman, put the question to the mom: "Tell me honestly," he said, "What means more to you and your husband. Is it going out

Friday night and having a few drinks to forget the week or is it your family—especially your little girl?" "Why! We love our daughter," came the mother's protest. "What does she mean, we don't care about her! We've given her everything."

Sounds familiar, doesn't it? It certainly does to me. In fact I've said it myself. I've even tried it myself. Giving things. But what kids want and need is something different. Something very different.

But it's so hard. It's hard even to have kids, especially teenage kids. Nobody should ever have to be a teenager.

And it's so hard, really, to be a parent. It's hard to be a friend to kids. They bug you so. They know your weak spots. They know just how to hurt you! And sometimes you want to punch 'em in the nose, or worse!

And they're so clever at making you lose your cool. They make you blow it—to blow the whole family thing. And then you feel so guilty. So what do you do? How do you love your kids?

Not that it was ever easy back in pre-suburban times or pre-"hysteric" times or pre-affluent times or pre-country club times or pre-weekend-party times or even in first-century times.

Apparently it was far from easy, for Paul has a word about just this problem in the first century, which was important enough for a pretty powerful paragraph in his letter to the Christians in Ephesus.

What he says is, "And now a word to you parents. Don't keep on scolding and nagging your children, and making them angry and resentful. Rather, bring them up with the loving discipline the Lord Himself approves, with suggestions and Godly advice." There ought to be something there to help us.

For one thing, Paul says don't be the cause of your children's anger. "Don't keep on scolding and nagging your children," he says, "making them angry and resentful."

Of course our reaction is, "Don't scold my kids? What do you mean? Cop out on my whole responsibility as a parent? Let the kids walk all over me? Have their own way? Grow up as spoiled brats? — Not on your life! I'm the parent, they're the kids. I'm supposed to discipline and correct and teach them."

I don't think the Lord would argue with our responsibility to do just that. Of course we must discipline our kids! But how and in what spirit? What, for instance, is our responsibility for our children's behavior? Could it be that sometimes we do make them angry and that we do cause them to resent us? We do it very often not only in our scolding and nagging, but also in our "keeping on" scolding and nagging. We sometimes become excessively critical and essentially negative in our whole relationship with our children.

Transactional Analysis tells us that the child in all of us tends to feel *not okay*—to feel judged and to feel like a bad person, an unacceptable person, a person always on trial, always being judged, and always "under the gun."

This doesn't mean there aren't times for being negative. For there are times for being angry—for letting a kid know he's hurt us, disappointed us, or has done something dangerous to himself or others. But we should not harbor it. And we should not "let the sun go down upon our anger," as Paul so beautifully put it.

But have you noticed how positive Jesus always was with children? "Let the little children come unto Me," He said, "and forbid them not." He took the kid's side in opposition to the adults who viewed kids as an inconvenience. He said "If you, being evil, know how to do good things for your children, how much more will your heavenly Father do . . .?" God always wants to give good things to His children, to shower them with His blessings. He wants us to bless our kids, too—to give them joy, laughter, happy times, and to share the best we have and are with them, especially our love.

Kids are real people. They are just as much hurt by insults and by the big put-down as we are. Do you think we could take being put down as often as our kids take it from us?

So many things. So hard. I'd do anything to take back some of those years, some of those moments, and some of those words with my children. What a hurt. And I never meant it to be that way. Most of us don't. But what we do and say often isn't really what, in our deepest heart, we mean.

But it builds. It lies there sleeping. It is stacking up there against us. And one day it falls on us. One day it hurts too much—and the storm of our petty wrath comes sweeping back on us from our children: in anger, in hurt, in out-cries of stored venom, or even in physical violence. Or it comes in some quiet denial, some self-destruction—like smoking grass or taking dope or drinking booze.

And we're aghast. And if we see at all, it is so late. Sometimes it's too late.

"Don't keep on scolding and nagging your kids," Paul says, "making them angry and resentful." After all, they are people. They hurt too. Stand in their shoes. Accept them. Love them. Build them up. The world throws enough at them without our being their enemies too.

"Rather," Paul says, "bring them up with loving discipline the Lord Himself approves." Give them strong love. That's what he's saying. That's also what Jesus says in many ways in the Gospels. Tough love—that's the way to go. Not soupy sentimentalism. Don't be an emotional slob. Don't be weak and wishy-washy. Have integrity in your love. Have strength in it. Give your kids something to hold on to!

We perhaps are tempted to make love something weak—to see it as emotional feeling and the physical expression of that feeling. I often hear parents describe the way they express affection for their kids by reporting "I 'loved' them." And what they mean is that they held them. They kissed them. They hugged them.

Now, that is a beautiful thing. But it isn't love. It's an expression of love. Love is a relationship. Love is believing in someone. Love is seeing into the heart of another person. Love is understanding who a person really is—and appreciating it, honoring it, and building it up in that person. I think love is saying, "Hey! You're someone special. You're different. You're unique. I respond to who you are. I *love* you."

There are some hang-ups in my life that I believe my parents (bless their hearts anyway) have passed on to me, and I'm stuck with them. But one thing about my father was never ever in doubt. He loved me. He used to tell me about my life—who I was and what my qualities were. He affirmed that. He built me up. I still remember walking along through the snow when I was a small boy, crossing the street not far from our house, with my father holding my hand and saying, "You love people, Arthur. You feel things. The second generation is always better than the first. You'll be a better minister than I am."

I knew my father as an aggressive, competitive, and self-made man. So his saying that surprised me. I was touched by the humility, the self-effacing quality of his spirit. I was touched that he believed in me, that he thought I was going to do something good in the world—and even do it better than he.

"If you love someone," the apostle Paul says, "You will be loyal to him no matter what the cost. You will always believe in him, always expect the best of him, and always stand your ground in defending him."

What an honor to be believed in by your father. Maybe that's the "loving discipline" our text speaks of, "that the Lord Himself approves." Discipline is discipleship, following, hanging tough, and not giving up. And maybe "loving discipline" is being loved into following and believed into persevering, trying, and growing. But maybe loving discipline is also teaching someone else, by example with infinite caring, those qualities of following, humility, and trying.

Maybe for me, it's passing it on to my youngest son, Andrew. Maybe it's giving him a dream to dream about himself, like being a disciple like Andrew of old—one who was humble enough to go and get his brother and bring him to the Lord, and then to fade into the background.

Perhaps the loving part of discipline is the hardest part. It's hard to teach by humility: by daring to show even your kid, your son, that you're human and that you're weak. Maybe there's nothing greater a child can learn than that his father is not God—but a man. To show that sometimes he, too, is afraid or selfish or tired or sinful—and is sorry, and needs to ask forgiveness.

Tough love is strong enough to say, "I'm weak." "I'm afraid." "I need you." "And I need God."

Many of our fathers did that for us. Mine still does. How great to do the same for our children.

And, then, always remember this for your sons and daughters: give them Christian counsel. After trying not be the cause of your children's anger and trying to give them strong love—do all you can to make sure you give them Christian counsel. "Bring them up," Paul says, "with suggestions and Godly advice."

We sure have plenty of suggestions for our kids, haven't we! But I'm not sure how Godly our advice is. I suppose our greatest temptation is to say to our kids, no matter what their age, "You're gonna do this because I say you're gonna do it." And we say this with no explanation and no reason. It's so easy when you're tired and living on the nervous edge to fling out, "My will be done, you idiots." We're so insensitive. But we all know better. No matter how educated we are or how broad our experience or how high our station, we do it. And we live to regret it.

Give "suggestions and Godly advice." Talk to your kids. Converse with them. Give them reasons. Point out alternatives. That's what God says. And He says, "Tell them what I want them to know!"

Well—what does God want them to know? Look at the Bible. Look at the Sermon on the Mount. Look at the Four Gospels. These are full of advice—Godly advice—straight from Jesus. And it's given in Jesus' way—so gently, with stories and analogies. Even with people who were obstinate and unlovable, Jesus was patient. And apparently Jesus did a lot of listening.

Study Jesus and learn how to talk, especially with kids. The Scripture says of Him, "He will not shout nor raise His voice in the market place." Jesus was very quiet, very gentle, and very uncondemning—whether He was with the woman taken in adultery or with Zacchaeus who had cheated the people to line his pockets or with the rich young man who couldn't meet the challenge and went away sorrowful. Jesus let the rich young man go. He doesn't push. He doesn't even push us to conversion. "Behold, I stand at the door and knock," He says. "If anyone hears My voice and opens the door I will come in to him." He's just waiting for us to be ready.

We could be that way to our children. But when they're ready, what do we say? What would God want us to say? My guess is that it's different from the favorite bits of advice from the world, which we so readily offer. Why not read the Bible and see how you should be advising your kids. Read Proverbs. Read the Sermon on the Mount in Matthew 5-7. Read the Ten Commandments again. Read all the advice in Paul's letters.

Tell your kids about sex, for instance. We may think we're a liberated generation—but that's not what I hear, in my work with kids and in my marriage counseling, about what parents are saying. The parents of these young people are very uptight, very much afraid of sex, and too frightened to be very open. Most of us are afraid to talk about the real stuff. And our kids need to know before they're into it. And they need to know it from a Christian view.

And what about those other things? What about alcohol, drugs, conscientious objection to war, and choosing a vocation? What about friendships and working hard? What about faith? Our kids need to know.

And we can't tell them until we first have struggled with these questions ourselves, wrestled honestly with what the Bible says about them, sincerely prayed, and really come up with something. We have too many opinions for which we don't have very good reasons, and the kids see straight through that. And we do too many things we really haven't thought through as Christians. There would be far less alcohol and social drinking in our Christian homes, for instance, if we had honestly thought and prayed it through—particularly in light of the drug culture we're in today.

Those kids are watching our lives. They're checking out how we live as well as what we say. And the biggest single obstacle to the teaching of Christ's way to children is the inconsistent and sometimes hypocritical lives of parents. And that includes my life, too. I've shouted. I've advised one thing and done another. And I've sometimes been openly chided by my shrewd kids with a quotation from one of my own sermons. We're condemned by our own mouths so often.

But let me tell you that the sooner you help your kids to be Christians, by actual conversion, the sooner they'll be nice to you, understanding of you, and compassionate toward you. And you will be able to have real conversations and be able to talk quietly, creatively, constructively, and conclusively. And you'll have more fun. They'll be better friends. And you will be a better friend to them.

The most Godly advice that you can give your kids is "Turn your life to the Lord." "Give your heart to Jesus." "Be His child."

The most important point is that this beautiful thing will happen most surely for your kids when you make sure is has happened first for you. Christ needs your heart first. And then, watch out for the good and great things that will happen to those kids you love so much.

LET'S DISCUSS

1. *Is it possible to love your child in a way that isn't really love at all? How about your love for your kids?*

2. *How is "scolding and nagging" different from loving discipline?*

3. *How can you discipline a child without being the cause of his anger?*

4. *How can we love and understand our kids and be on their side before it is too late?*

5. *Does your love for another person respond to how unique and beautiful they are? Does your love affirm and support them?*

6. *Do you find it easy to believe in your son or daughter? Do they know you believe in them?*

7. Do your children really know how human you
   are — that you are not God?

8. What kind of advice do you give your children? Is
   it a lot of opinion or is it "Godly" advice?

9. Have you checked out how you live recently, as
   an example to your children?

10. Do you dare to help your kids turn their lives to
    the Lord?

How to Love Your Parents

In the hospital room of a ninety-year-old lady who was dying, I sat for a time with her daughter, a woman of perhaps sixty years. The mother, who had been vital and alive and laughing and full of conversation only days before, had slipped into a coma. She was dying. The daughter, herself a mother and grandmother, could hardly speak. Her eyes filled with tears.

I've thought about her many times since then. And I have thought about many other middle-aged sons or daughters whom I've been with at the time of their parent's death. The world encourages us to say things like, "Oh, it was expected." "No problem." "Mother had a good, long life." "She was old and very sick." "We knew it was coming." "Just one of those things."

But I'm not convinced that it's really that easy. I believe that when a parent dies, it's a hurt and a heartache no matter how old you are. Because it's something like no other relationship in life when you're somebody's kid—when there's somebody in this world who is your mother or father: who once long ago brought you into the world and held you in their arms; who cooked meals for you and bought clothes for you; who gave you warmth, a roof, a table, and a bed; who sent you to kindergarten and later to college; who loved you, prayed for you, and cried for you. That's really something that you cannot help but remember. No matter how embarrassed you may be about your dottering old parent or how angry you may feel about some of the stupid, unthinking things he or she may have done long ago or how lousy a parent you may think he or she is—when you're middle-aged, and your mother or father dies and you suddenly realize you're not anybody's little kid anymore . . . oh, that's very sad and not a little lonely.

It's so easy to be embarrassed by parents: to knock them, to put them down, or to apologize for them no matter what age you are. Especially when you're growing up and are a teenager, you know just what parents ought to be like. This was evident to me as a father on a summer Sabbatical trip in Europe when all seven of us in our family were traveling by car together. The kids, we discovered, had invented a word which they were whispering loudly under their breaths at places like public restaurants, at border customs, and almost anywhere that father tried to speak in the native language or explain something to a waiter or get directions or tell a joke. The word, in their secret language of vivid descriptions, was *curfley*, which means, "Eeek! I want to go through the floor!" "How can my parents be so stupid?" "I want to get out of here." "I don't even know these characters." Fortunately, it was usually accompanied by enough tittering and laughter to suggest that it was not said in desperate seriousness.

And yet, parents are somehow "there." We really sort of belong to them. We somehow cannot escape them. So how do you come to terms with parents? Putting it bluntly, how can we love our parents?

There are some very simple things in the Bible about how to do that. It says first, "Obey them." "Children," Paul writes to the Christian kids in Ephesus, "obey your parents; this is the right thing to do because God has placed them in authority over you."

Already sounds ominous, doesn't it.? Those awful words are there: *authority*, and *obey*. Sounds a lot like, "Do it!" or like "Follow my orders." It's like prison or the army or summer camp or some other awful place.

It's interesting that the Bible doesn't say, either here or in the Ten Commandments, "Love your parents" or "Be nice to your folks because they love you." That seems strange when you stop to think how crucial love is to us—how profoundly love is so often the issue between us and our parents, how total is our concern for love, how much we talk about love, and how desperately we ache to be loved.

That's what a desperate little girl who had tried to take her life said to me in the hospital later: "My parents don't love me. They don't care. They never have loved me. They never will."

You know that most parents do love their child. But their love asks something of their kid. It says, "Here are some things we think you should do." "Here's a way of life that at least for now will be good for you." "We feel school is important if you're to make it in the world." "We feel being in off the streets at night studying and then sleeping is better for you now—for your health and for your growing up." "We want to help you, to prepare you."

And how kids can bristle at that! "What if I don't want to do all those respectable middle-class things?" "What if I want a 'life-style' of my own?" "Maybe drugs do something for me." "Maybe my friends are better for me than you think." "Besides, what makes you think you know so much—you're out of it in your middle-aged world." "You don't know what's really happening anymore!" "If you really love me you'd let me do what I want to do!"

Is that really love's way with a young person? Is that really how you show love for someone, especially your own child, by not teaching him or her, by not offering guidance, or by not taking the chance of getting on the wrong side of the loved one by offering advice or disagreeing? Standing by and letting someone who you love be hurt maybe isn't love at all. Maybe love really can't ever be proven on the basis of concessions or big gifts or discipline or pretending that a thirteen-year-old is ready to live the life of a thirty-year-old.

Love will come. Love is God's gift. Love is wherever God is. And if Jesus is Lord of a home, love will be there. In spite of anger, misunderstanding, terrible hurt, awful mistakes made by parents, and deep resentment harbored by kids —love will have its way. It isn't defeated that easily.

Maybe the Bible gives us something a lot harder to do than love—maybe something that even makes the right kind of love possible—and that is obedience. And this is for children. We are always our parents' children, but we are not always children. We do not always have to obey them. When we're little and growing up there are many people and rules we have to obey. It's for our own safety. It's for to learn, to grow, to know the rules, to avoid danger, to know the facts, and to build wisdom. We're not very wise at five or six, or even at fifteen or sixteen. Growing up is very gradual. Somebody's got to hold on to us. Somebody has to play out the line—to let us go farther and farther afield and yet still hold on.

Perhaps in a world of teachers, policemen, bullies in the schoolyard, and all kinds of dangers and threats to our lives, it's not a bad thing to have at least two of the people we obey in this world be our parents. They're somebody in the world who have a stake in our destiny. They're somebody who love us because we're part of them. They're somebody who, even though they sometimes discipline us, teach us, and even berate and criticize us, would at a moment's notice go all the way to defend us or to save us even to losing their lives for us.

So obeying our parents isn't all one way. They pay too. They pay plenty. It's because they love us.

But the Bible claims something else from us in relation to our parents. We must honor them. "Honor your father and your mother," Paul writes to the young people of the Ephesus church. "This is the first of the Ten Commandments that ends with a promise."

Paul isn't writing off the Old Testament and the Ten Commandments. He is not saying, as we do, "Forget that Old Testament stuff: the wrath of God and all that bit. You don't have to take that seriously. Jesus—the liberator, the free spirit—has set us free from the law and all its obligations!"

The Commandments were serious business to

Paul, and he wasn't embarrassed to tell the kids to take them seriously, too. "Honor your father and mother."

Well, how do you do that? You mean a kid is supposed to say, "Yes sir," "no sir," "your obedient servant, ma'am," and bow and scrape and kow-tow and lick boots and be docile and silent and never talk back and always do what the parents say?

No, it doesn't mean that. But how about respecting them? How about recognizing who they are, and remembering that they just might be human like you and hurt in some ways they can't tell you. Maybe they don't get along very well with each other. They may need a little sympathy and a little understanding and a little compassion and a little kindness. Maybe they could use your prayers or your offer to help some way.

Have you ever walked in your parents' shoes? Have you ever thought what life is like for them? I wonder if a lot of kids—particularly teenage kids—never really felt it was their duty or obligation to put themselves in their parents' place: to think about what life may be like for them. "But," says the teenager, "aren't they supposed to be looking out for me and worrying about me and doing things for me? I mean, isn't it supposed to go the other way? Family life isn't supposed to be a bringing up parents deal, is it?"

Maybe it is, if you're a Christian or trying to be. And it was young Christians to whom Paul was writing. They were children of the church in Ephesus. If you're a Christian, maybe it's not such a tough assignment to care about and care for your folks.

There's a little guy at my house who sometimes doesn't even know what he's doing in his little acts of Christian caring. These are given so unblushingly, so genuinely. One Saturday night his father was lying on the living room couch shivering and aching under a blanket. All of a sudden there was the young prince standing beside his bed, leaning over and rubbing his back—and really doing it, so seriously, like a professional masseur! His father, I can tell you, was overcome by that act of such kindness, caring, and such obvious concern on his little son's part.

Honoring your parents, maybe, is just having a heart. It's respecting them, remembering that they have a life and a need and hopes and dreams and hurts and heartaches, too.

This is a good thing to remember when your parents are seventy-five or eighty-five. At that time they may be sick and not very strong anymore, or awfully lonely in a nursing home. Honoring is caring like Jesus would.

Therefore, obey them; honor them; and finally, live for them! Paul suggests there's a promise—a benefit or a reward—that goes along with honoring your parents. "And this is the promise," he says, "that if you honor your father and mother, yours will be a long life, full of blessing."

That's saying that honoring your parents has an effect upon your own life. Certain very positive things will be set in motion if you honor your parents, just as some very negative things will tend to intrude into your life if you dishonor your parents.

There are some kinds of revolutions and defiance that are courageous, good, noble, and make the world a better place. But there are others that are destructive. They destroy, undercut, and eat away at the revolutionary.

It's a very serious thing to live your whole life angry and unreconciled with your parents. Maybe it's like being unreconciled with yourselves —being at war with your own spirit, churned up inside, and having no peace in your hearts. Greatness comes out of confidence, as do assurance, unity, and faith. It's being right with yourself, right with God, being on target, and being "in the Spirit," if you will. And if you don't have that within yourself, you miss the power, and you fail.

By the same token, if you're jarring and out of phase and not at peace with your parents, you miss a power God intended you to have, and that also causes you to fail.

Our fathers and mothers are the roots of our lives. They are heritage, history, genetic trait, and physical strength. They are our foundation. They're a big part of what we're built upon. They're the launching pad for our flight into the soaring opportunities of life in our generation. And if our lives are not rightly connected with our parents, then instead of lift-off into life, we may have explosion and disaster. It's like the relay race. The baton has to be passed to another. We've got to break free to run our race, the particular race that God has given us—looking to Jesus. This means we can't run our parents' race, and they have no right to make us run theirs. But there is a unity of understanding, respect, and, in the deepest sense, *love*, which we can have that ultimately sets us free to be ourselves, yet taking with us the best that our parents have to offer.

We don't have to agree with our parents. I have deep theological, sociological, and political differences with my father. He thinks I'm crazy to believe in the devil, and I think he's sadly mistaken to be a Republican. But we love each other. He doesn't like my long hair any more than some of my parishioners used to—but there are things about me that he cares about that are more profound than hair. He's my father, my human creator. And I need his love, his support, and his caring in very much the way I need my Heavenly Father.

And there will always be a heritage I have from him: a love for history, a certain ambition, a keen competiveness, a certain physical, constitutional strength, low blood pressure, a full head of hair, a love for people, and, above all, a love for God. He gave that to me. It's priceless. And woe to me if I forget it!

Every one of our parents has given us something. Something we can be glad for. Something for which we can honor them. Our life is possible because of them.

If we remember that and keep learning from our fathers and mothers the best things they have to teach us, we'll be blessed in surprising ways. Maybe our lives will be longer. And maybe we'll be happier.

Maybe our parents' faith, morality, and ethics, though old-fashioned, are not as outdated and irrelevant as we sometimes think.

When they pray for us and are patient with us and keep on loving us, in spite of the ways we goof up (even as middle-agers), they're doing something very beautiful. It's something that Jesus Christ, the Lord of all lives and of all relationships,

90

has given them to do, for which we can be very glad. And it's something that perhaps we can do in a little better way for our children.

Obey your parents. Honor them. Live for them. And you'll be around a long time. You'll be happy. You'll be making the world a better place, not only in the power of your earthly mother and father, but also in the power of God, who loves us so much that for us He gave His Son to die on the cross, so that we could love Him and love each other. So we could even love our parents!

LET'S DISCUSS

1. How do you face the death of your parent? What does it mean for you?

2. Were your parents ever an embarrassment to you? Were you ever ashamed of them? How did you resolve that feeling?

3. How can you love your child and still teach him the things you think are best for him?

4. Is it your experience that obedience is viable — that parents can really ask that of their children?

5. What is honor for a parent? Is there a respect they deserve?

6. Can we care for parents the way Jesus would? Is it possible?

7. What effect does honoring your parents have on your own life?

8. How do you make peace with and get in tune with your parents? Is it important?

9. Have you thought about the heritage that your parents have given you?

10. What are the gifts of body and spirit that you have from your parents? Do you appreciate and honor your parents because of them? Might that really be a key to long life?

How to Love Your Brother

When you talk about loving different kinds of people as I have tried to do, you frequently have people stop you, even on the street, to suggest new subjects. One high school senior girl, who knew about fathers and mothers and husbands and wives, said, "That's okay and important but how about a word on 'how to love your brother and your sister'?" And I thought, "Good heavens! Haven't we covered that? Didn't that come in somehow under parents or kids or neighbor?" But on reflection it was very obvious that they're not the same, and that most of us have trouble with that special problem. How do you love your brother and your sister?

For many of us, brothers and sisters—physical, blood brothers and sisters—are a powerful part of our early upbringing. It was plainly a tense question for my young friend who made the suggestion. As I look back over my childhood and the years of my growing up with my brother and my two sisters, I have to admit that in those years it was a tense question for me. And, to my surprise, in some ways it still is. Brothers of forty don't necessarily stop competing with each other. Middle-aged siblings don't forget the feelings of their childhood and their youth. So, the brother-sister thing is a problem of childhood and adulthood as well.

But what about homes with brothers and sisters? What's it like, getting along together? Do most of us realize how many police calls—even in "nice," safe suburban towns—there are for what they call "domestic cases?" I wonder if we realize how violent many of those cases are. Often it's a knock-down, drag-out battle between husband and wife. But not always. Sometimes it's between kids. It's between brother and sister or brother and brother. Storms of anger that brew and boil like summer thunder are finally unleashed with savage violence.

Violence against brother and sister! How strange! People who've grown up since infants together, who've shared family love, happy times, and great memories together, are yet angry. Sometimes they're boiling mad with each other.

Maybe most of us don't bite or scratch or kick or pound, although I can clearly recall an awful day in my own childhood. At perhaps seven or eight years of age, in a horrible moment of anger, I took a belt to my brother, whipping him with the buckle. It was almost my last chance, for he was six feet, four inches tall already by age twelve. (He was six feet, six inches and 195 pounds during our college years.) We do have angers, strange feelings of hurt, resentment, hate, and rebellion against our brothers and sisters that loom up in the midst of our real love. And we don't know what to do with them.

My brother and I have been in competition ever since we were born. We're only fourteen months apart. We went to the same boy's prep school and the same men's college at about the same time. Later, at different times, we attended the same theological seminary. It seemed that everything I could do he could do better. Even in the things that were peculiarly and privately mine, he came along and did "my thing," doing circles around me in the process. The only athletic thing I was ever good at was rowing. For two years, I managed to be co-captain of my prep school crew and later was captain of the Harvard Freshman Crew. But along came my brother—six-foot, six-inch football end for three years in prep school, basketball center for four years, crack quarter-miler in track, and a natural athlete. In college he said: "Gee, what a fun thing Arthur's into," and went out for crew, ultimately rowing on Harvard's Varsity Crew (even rowing against Cambridge University of England) while I, for three years, stroked the second university crew.

I had to swallow my pride. I still do. Even in the theological ministerial game, he's the professor and I'm the country parson.

So it isn't just when you're a kid or a teenager that you may have problems with a brother or sister. You can have mixed feelings about those kinds of people all through your life.

What then do you do about them? How do you love your brother—or your sister?

Jesus' answer is, *"Make peace with your brother."* This is a test of your faith.

Isn't the special problem of relationships between brothers and sisters the fact that they could go on unresolved, forever? It's because you think you know your brother or sister so well. After all, you've got a whole stack of evidence against him.

You can remember incidents way back to four years old that just prove what a malicious, selfish, and irritating person he or she is! I've even got a list like that about my little sister. She's very arch and arty, and she swings in the European opera-theater-television-concert set. Sometimes I think she's just "too - too!" "But, of course," I tell myself, "she always was that way!" When we were children and had rooms next door to each other on the third floor of the old rambling parsonage in Portsmouth, New Hampshire, she had papered her whole room —walls, ceiling, everything—with pictures of movie stars. And, of course, as a middle-western preachy-person, I'm just a freak to her. She has always thought I was too pious. She used to taunt me in my seminary days about my being anti-alcohol.

And now I never see her. She's an ocean away. Our lives are passing: I'm forty-five and look it and she's forty-two and doesn't look it. But, it's going, going, and someday it will be gone. And sometimes I wonder where we will be—me and my little sister.

It would be so easy just to keep on thinking of her in terms of all the little stereotypes of years ago. But that really isn't fair. That really isn't where she is. That even isn't who she is.

We have to make peace. Actually my own faith is at stake. So is yours. Jesus says:

> If, when you are bringing your gift to the altar, you suddenly remember that your brother has a grievance against you, leave your gift where it is before the altar. First, go and make peace with your brother, and only then come back and offer your gift.

Our faith itself is in danger if we are not "right"

with the blood brothers and sisters of our own families. After all, God gave them for us to love. If we can't have peace and understanding and honest communication there, what good will we be for making peace in Indonesia, Ireland, Israel, or in the ghettoes of America? Jesus makes it very clear we just can't let it sit there for a lifetime, eating away at us.

That doesn't mean we have to like our brother or sister to accept everything he or she does and is. Some things we never could be able to accept and still remain true to ourselves—to be our own person or Jesus' person.

My little sister, for instance, doesn't really buy Jesus Christ and His church for herself. But that doesn't keep me from loving her. At least, it had better not. I need to try to understand. I need to try to make peace.

Without that, we are to some degree destroying ourselves. Anger, even misunderstanding, is self-destructive. Jesus even says it's a sin. He says we can be punished for it.

> Anyone who nurses anger against his brother must be brought to judgment. If he abuses his brother he must answer for it to the court. If he sneers at him he will have to answer for it, in the fires of hell.

Long-held anger, of course, hurts us. But it also hurts our brother. Who does he have in life to believe in him, to encourage him, and to understand him, if he doesn't have us? Everyone needs a last line of defense—the last person you can go to when all else fails and when nobody else understands. When the whole world is against you or when even your husband or wife couldn't help you or when your kids wouldn't understand, or when your father and mother would maybe be too shocked to do any good—that's when, if you've got a brother or sister you can talk to, you've got something that is very precious in this world. It's having someone who, when the chips are down, will just listen and will not judge or condemn or even give a lot of bad advice. It's a weapon God meant all His children to have in the arsenal of their defense.

And for all the differences in my family, I thank God I have that special defense and help and strength in my brother. I will never forget one dark night in my life not so many years ago. I was lying in a hospital bed looking out across the city from my fifth floor room and saw its lights through tears. I hurt. Not just in my back where I'd had surgery, but in my heart, too. There was near-despair in my soul. And I telephoned all the way across the country to my "little" brother, and poured it all out to him. He's the same guy I'd fought with as a boy. All he did, really, was listen. But he was my brother. There was nobody else like him in all the world. There was no one else to whom I could have told what I had to tell him that night. Only to my brother could I tell that.

Brothers and sisters are a gift. Make peace with them. Someday your very life and faith may depend on it.

There is something else that might help in loving our brothers and our sisters. And that is: *Look for the Holy Spirit in your brother.* A curious juxtaposition in Mark's Gospel, just before Jesus' confrontation with His mother and brothers who had come looking for Him—essentially to get Him home to Nazareth for a rest cure—is Jesus' most powerful teaching about the respect we are supposed to have for the Holy Spirit. He said with vehemence,

> I tell you this, no sin, no slander, is beyond forgiveness for men; *but, whoever slanders the Holy Spirit can never be forgiven;* he is guilty of eternal sin.

And Mark's comment is,

> He said this because they had declared that He was possessed by an unclean spirit.

Jesus had been accused, by the Temple representatives and by the doctors of the law, of working for the powers of evil. They were so jealous of the power of good and of God working in Jesus that they stooped not only to character assassination but also to trying to destroy the power of the Holy Spirit in Him by telling the people that the power in Him was the working of the devil, of evil spirits, and of demonic powers.

Jesus' mother and brothers were saying essentially the same thing. "You're crazy, man! You're out of your head. You're possessed. No man does what you do—leaving a good job and home and friends and family and going off preaching and setting himself up as a healer!—Come to your senses, man! Don't you remember? You're our big brother Jesus. Your scene is Nazareth. You're a country carpenter, not a big-city doctor! Come on, brother, this just doesn't fit. We just can't see you in this healing, public preaching, crowd-leading deal. You're out of your element. You're over your head. Come on home where you belong!"

Those boys from home had missed the significance of their brother's life. They didn't see what He was really about. And not only did they not understand what He was good for and what His vocation ought to be, but they believed He was sick. They thought He'd lost His mind, that He'd lost His balance and become a fanatic. They concluded that the evil spirits of pride and greed and public aggrandizement had gone to His head and had taken over His heart.

They had missed the point. They couldn't believe that someone so familiar to them—especially someone in their own family—could be a great man, a chosen man, and God's man. This narrow, restricted, and unimaginative view we might well have shared about Jesus, but, unfortunately, we all too easily share this view also about our own brothers and sisters.

Here was miracle: the Holy Spirit of God, the very Person of God, had come into their midst. But they were too full of prejudices, preconceived ideas, envies, and jealousies to see the real heart of their brother. And don't we do the same? We look for God's Spirit to be present everywhere but close at hand, and can hardly believe it might be there right in front of us in the life of our own flesh and blood brother or sister!

The poets keep warning us that it is:

> Not where the wheeling systems darken
> And our benumbed conceiving soars! —
> The drift on pinions, would we hearken,
> Beats at our own clay-shuttered doors.
>
> The angels keep their ancient places; —
> Turn but a stone and start a wing!
> 'Tis ye, 'Tis your estranged faces,
> That miss the many-splendored thing.

Jesus says it's sin to miss that "many-splendored thing" when it is the Holy Spirit in the heart and life of our brother. He was stung by it in His life —that His own brothers had not seen God in Him and had dared to call that spirit within Him an evil spirit. And that, He said, is the one sin in all the world that is unforgivable—*unforgivable!*

In other words, woe to us if we do not appreciate our brother or sister. Woe to us if we fail to see God's Spirit in their lives. As George Fox and the Quakers would have said, "to see that of God within him." Christians are supposed to recognize the Holy Spirit, to recognize truth, light, and love in other people—and especially in those closest to us.

And what a breakthrough when we come to recognize that the brother whom we envy or resent or feel anger toward is, in fact, a child of God—a son of the King, a gifted person whom God loves and in whom He dwells. When we see that, our brother suddenly becomes a whole new person to us. He is someone we can thank God for, someone we can reach out to and love—in spite of his being our brother.

So we'd better not sell our brother or sister short. Look for the Holy Spirit in your brother.

Then, this last word to help us. *Recognize your brothers and sisters in Christ.* We have blood brothers and sisters for a purpose. They're a beautiful gift from God. We should do everything in our power to live at peace with them. And looking for the Spirit of God within them will help us to love them and see the best in them and be a worthy brother or sister to them. But what if you have no blood brother or sister? Or what if every effort and overture on your part fails, and there's still a hurt in that relationship? Or what if your blood brothers and sisters live halfway across the country, and because they aren't around, they cannot walk with you, stand by you, and share your life with you?

The exciting thing is that God provides us with brothers and sisters anyway: the most beautiful kind of brothers and sisters. These are the ones He gives us in the Christian fellowship. They are ours in the Spirit. They are brothers and sisters in Christ who belong to us in the family of the faith. This is the church, the brothers and sisters who surround us each Sunday morning.

They're not just any indiscriminate or happenstance conglomeration of people. They're not just chance visitors on a given Sunday morning. They are a special group of people who have prayed for each other, have loved each other, and who have suffered with each other. They have stood at hospital bedsides together, laughed together, and held hands and hearts together. They hope together as dear friends with a special bond.

Little wonder that Jesus could say on that day when His blood brothers stood outside the door asking Him to come out:

> Who are My brothers? And looking around at those who were sitting in the circle about Him He said, "Here are My mother and My brothers. Whoever does the will of God is My brother, My sister, My mother!"

Wow! An instant family, with instant brothers and sisters. This is something no other institution, no other organization, and no other community or society offers. It is something not even the most exclusive fraternities and sororities can offer. It's a brotherhood in Christ, a brotherhood of believers, and a brotherhood of sinners. They are people who know about suffering, who know about loneliness, who know about pain, and who know about sin. Yet they are those who love you, not because you've proven yourself or because you're good or admirable or likeable, but just because you're God's child. That's the way they are. You each are a redeemed child, a "prodigal" child. You each are a forgiven, healed child who's found a hope, and who's sharing that hope by wrapping all the other brothers and sisters in arms of love and concern.

Wouldn't you say that's good medicine for life? Wouldn't you agree that it is reason for going on and for not giving up and for hanging in there? It is reason for running the race of life and pressing on toward the mark of the high calling of God in Christ Jesus. It is a company and a comradeship that makes it all worthwhile, fun, good, and deep. It is deep as the heart.

I had breakfast once with a dear young friend of mine in his home, which included his wife and little son and his father and mother. We took hands for the blessing, and his father asked him to pray. In that beautiful, heartfelt prayer was one phrase I will never forget. It was, "God bless brother Arthur." With years between us, yet we were brothers. This was true because through tears and troubles and prayer and the Spirit's power, Jesus our Lord had made us brothers.

These are good reasons, don't you think, to be brothers and sisters—in the spirit of the One who died on a cross long ago to be our Savior and Lord, our friend and our brother?

LET'S DISCUSS

1. *Has the problem of loving your own brother or sister ever been a real one for you?*

2. If so, was it only in childhood or did it become an occasional problem to cope with in your adult life?

3. Have you ever seen real healing later on in life of the hurts and competitiveness of children in their childhood?
   (a) Has it worked for you?
   (b) Would you like it to work for you?
   (c) Would you let it work for you?

4. What is "making peace" with your brother? Does it have something to do with your faith? Could your failure to "make peace" with a brother or sister adversly affect your own faith or even destroy it?

5. Why, for your health's and sanity's sake, do you need a brother or sister?

6. Have you ever seen the Holy Spirit in your own brother or sister, or have they seen Him in you?

7. Would the Spirit's presence in a man tend to make his life different and more attractive to you? How?

8. Are you able to see that Spirit in those close to you?

9. How real is your "brotherhood in Christ" feeling with your fellow Christians in your church or in some other group?

10. What is an "instant brother"?

How to Love Your Neighbor

Two unusual letters once reached me on the same day, both of which were wistful reminders to me of the poignant reality of man's basic separation today from other men. They reminded me of how fleeting life is, and of how temporary and transitory relationships between human beings have become these days.

One was from a young businessman in California with whom I'd had dinner a week or two before. He was writing from a hotel room in San Francisco where he was catching up on his work, listening to organ music, and incidentally sharing with me how much great music had reassurred him once again of God's love. He wrote:

> Your visit was most welcome and appreciated.

And then he said,

> Our mobile society leaves us grasping in space and in time for those we love and respect—but so be it.

For him this was a frustration, but it also was an acceptance of life in a world of broken family bonds and of fleeting relationships with friends. But it's so sad. And it's where most of us are.

The other letter, just a card, was from a woman I had seen only with a touch and a hurried glance over the shoulder at coffee hour at church the Sunday before. I had not seen her since the time of her husband's recent death. She walked with a certain sorrow in those days. She wrote:

> Today while my back was turned, somebody reassuredly grasped my arm unexpectedly. It was you. It was just the extra "something" I needed. Thanks a lot.

Only a moment. Only a hurried instant in a whirlwind of hurtling events and passing time. But it meant something.

Both notes said: That's the way it is. That's the way life is. And I agree with them. It is that way, and we can't change it. We have to live with it. But even though it is that way—so fast fleeing by, so impermanent—we nevertheless have to give ourselves to others in it. We have to invest something in it as it goes rocketing by. We have to do our loving thing in that unstable and unpredictable context. Whatever we're going to be and whatever we're going to give of love, we have to do it in the fragile, fleeting seconds that are all that's given to us on this rocketing ride into the future of this modern life.

There is so little time anymore to touch anybody. There are so few moments to hug and to hold on. There are only a few unsteady seconds for stopping to look anyone straight in the eye.

It's hard enough in such a world to hold on to our primary relationships, with the ones to whom we owe the most. They deserve the deepest duty and the highest obligation. It's hard enough these days to love a wife, a husband, a kid, or a parent. How, for heaven's sake, can we possibly love the world—and particularly our "neighbor" in that world?

Anyone have any idea? The Bible has, and Jesus spells it out in the beautiful story we all love from Luke's Gospel. A man was robbed on his way down to Jericho. He was left in a ditch. A minister on his way to do hospital calling had too many good works to do to have time to stop. A Levite on his way to a committee meeting had too many more important things to do than stop. Only a man of the kind nobody liked took time to stop and help. "Who was the neighbor?" Jesus asked. It was the guy who wasn't too busy or too important, the one who took time and stopped and gave.

It is so easy to find ourselves in that scene. And it's usually not as the "Good Samaritan." That story is a challenge, even a desperate, critical challenge to Christians. How, after all, do you love your neighbor?

That's a very embarrassing question. I find it hard to love my neighbors. It is not because I don't like them. It is not because we have nothing in common. It is not because I'm crass and don't care. It is simply that my neighbor and I are too busy for each other. We never see each other. He does his thing and I do mine. We don't even know each other very well. What we say is that we haven't time to love our neighbor. No time. No time.

One neighbor of mine is president of the Munsingwear Corporation, and we meet only occasionally when he walks his dog late at night. Another sells products for General Mills and is building another house on the beautiful St. Croix River, some fifty miles away. We say "hi" as we leave in the morning or return for dinner. My young friend, the Honeywell salesman next door, greets me when we are both heading out into the day from our respective back doors: "Hi, Bob!"—"Hi, Art!" But that's pretty much it. Nothing deep. Nothing heavy. And it kills me that I do not really know my neighbors.

But then I read Luke's Gospel and hear what Jesus says about neighbors, and suddenly I see something very interesting. It begins to dawn on me that the challenge to be a neighbor isn't really about the people next door at all, although I cannot write off my obligation to them that easily. But I find that, oddly enough, the call to be a neighbor is specifically a call to the man on the move. "But a Samaritan," the Scripture says, "who was making a journey came upon him, and when he saw him was moved to pity."

This has got to mean that it is exactly the busy man-about-town and man-about-the-world— who's here today, and in New York or San Francisco or Chicago or Houston or Peru or London or Paris tomorrow—who is called to be a neighbor. The fast-moving man on the run is not exempt. Because our neighbor, according to Jesus, is the man we find in need when we are most busy, when we're going somewhere important with big things to do, and when we don't have much time. It's just when we think our life and business are too significant and essential for the future of the world for us to be involved with anything so mundane and lowly. It's when we're tempted to protest along with Robert Frost, "But I have promises to keep, and miles to go before I sleep, and miles to go before I sleep."

Our neighbor is the guy we don't have time for,

the fellow "out there" in the world. He is very often not a person we know. He may be one who nobody knows. He is the person who isn't at home and who isn't safe in familiar surroundings among people he loves. He's a stranger, a traveler, a face in the crowd. He's the passing world—that ship in the night who passes us in the dark and to whom we signal once or twice before he is gone.

I think Jesus is saying to us: "Hey, busy people—there's your man! He's sitting beside you on the airplane. He's across from you in the lobby. He's your competitor. He's your boss. She's the new little frightened secretary. He's the neighbor kid you've heard is into drugs. He's the guy in the company who's doing too much drinking. He's your partner in the firm who has a girl on the side. He's your friend who's cheating and thinks he's getting away with it.

"And," Jesus says, "He is the fellow who's going to mess up your schedule if you stop to talk to him and take time to listen to him and bother to get involved in his need. And he's precisely the one I want you to help. He's the one I want you to talk to and to encourage and to whom I want you to tell the Good News of love."

What an assignment! He might even be there on the ski slopes when you've at last managed to get away for a few days with the family. He might be anywhere. Any inconvenient "where."

Can we love that kind of neighbor? Jesus says we can, no matter how busy we are or how fast we're moving or how exalted and important we may be.

The kind of love for neighbor to which Jesus is calling Christians is an immediate, costly, and caring kind of love. Remember what the Samaritan did?

> He went up and bandaged his wounds, bathing them with oil and wine. Then he lifted him onto his own beast, brought him to an inn, and looked after him there. Next day he produced two silver pieces and gave them to the innkeeper, and said, "Look after him, and if you spend anymore, I will repay you on my way back."

Interesting, isn't it. What if the story had gone like this:

> Seeing the man he said to himself, "This is a serious social problem. And the real issue is: how safe is the Jericho road going to be for future travelers if robbers are allowed to do this sort of thing? It's a matter of police protection, but also—obviously—of the social disorientation and personal frustration of the people who became robbers. Now, to be relevant we've really got to think of the long-range solution to the deep, underlying social problems of this country. We certainly don't want to have a merely do-gooder, band-aid sort of approach. I'm going to see that a study of this whole Jericho road situation is made immediately. We'll get a report into the legislature so that the government can act responsibly. And perhaps some private social agencies will want to help, too. Of course it may take awhile. But in the end we'll be doing far more good than a quick half-cocked, not well-thought-out, little old lady in tennis shoes, typical old-fashioned, do-gooder, and Christian churchy approach could do. Sorry, of course, about this particular chap, but it's the saving of the large numbers in the future that's important."

But the "good Samaritan" didn't say that. He was terribly old-fashioned. He just didn't seem to know that you need to study the situation first before you move in to help. He didn't realize that, if possible, you involve as many people as you can and in the end get government funding as the only way to go.

Jesus was talking about immediate action, about acting out of the emotion of the heart and out of pity and out of caring—right now! Also, He was talking about maybe even paying through the nose, to put up money and to let your act of kindness cost you something,

These are the very things that modern, sophisticated, and institutionalized Christians have learned to scoff at and to beware of. Get an organization to do it, is our cry. One man can't make any difference alone. The goody-good Christians have done that one-arm, temporary thing for far too long!

Maybe the instinctive, straight-from-the-heart, high-priced response to human need, with great risk involved, is something that more of us need to be ready for and willing to have as our style—our *modus operandi*.

After all, we're so programmed. We do have places to go. We have got huge responsibilities. And yet, maybe the Lord knows we need to be sensitive enough to see human need right when it's occurring and not to be afraid to risk our whole schedule to meet it. The Holy Spirit sometimes does unusual things with the life and daily schedule of a Christian, if he will let Him. In His own way, the Holy Spirit reorganizes our day and takes care of the connections we don't make —particularly if we're following Him and trying to respond to Him.

The Samaritan gave from his heart. He met the need. He took the time. It happened right in the middle of his journey. He probably had a business meeting he was trying to get to. But he saved the life of one single son of God by the side of road.

Is there anybody by the side of your road? I've had them. And I'm ashamed of my straight-ahead eyes and my faster walk and my heavy foot on the gas. And yet, when I have stopped, I've been so grateful. Good things have happened. And I believe God was in it.

One of my teenaged daughters once told me a tale that had just haunted her. It was reported by one of her teachers at school that the night before, on one of those straight, lonely stretches of Wyoming highway with thirty or forty miles between towns and the speed limit at 75-80 miles an hour, a man's car had run into trouble, and he had pulled to the side of the highway. The temperature was close to zero. He waved at the infrequently passing cars, desperately begging for a ride. But no one stopped. He had a gun in the car. The next morning the state highway patrol found his body beside the car where he had shot himself. Pinned to his coat was his own hand-written message of judgment on the world: "My car broke down. I waited here eleven hours trying to stop someone to help me. I was freezing to death. But no one would stop."

The help he needed was immediate, costly, and caring. Is that really too much for us?

The key is the quality of kindness. "Which of these three do you think was neighbor to the man who fell into the hands of the robbers?" Jesus asked. "The one who showed kindness," came the answer. And the Master's response was simply, "Go, and do as he did."

What He asks of us is so basic. Kindness. And that means seeing all human beings as worth something—as children of God and, therefore, as our brothers and sisters. It is caring about some-one.

The problem for most of us is that we decide secretly that some people are not as much worth caring about as others. We think some people are more important to us than others. This naturally limits us to people we know.

It's just possible that our concern should be about the people God knows. And He knows everybody. Therefore every person, potentially, has something of God in him that we need, and which needs us. We never know what passing stranger is somebody God has sent with a message or an experience for us. You never know who's going to be our "angel unawares."

A little Scottish poem says it:

> If after Kirk ye bide a wee,
> There's some would like to speak to ye;
> If after Kirk ye rise and flee,
> We'll all seem cold and stiff to ye.
> The one that's in the seat wi' ye,
> Is stranger here than you, may be;
> All here hae got their fears and cares —
> Add you your soul into our prayers;
> Be you our angel unawares.

Maybe there's a beautiful experience out there, waiting to happen to us—if we expect it and if we believe that God deals with His people that way and if we believe that His Holy Spirit actually does work through chance meetings and relationships that look like accidents but are, in fact, part of His plan.

Kindness is caring about people, loving people, and expecting beautiful things with people. It involves being open and eager and ready for anything with people.

I am one of the worst offenders against that ideal of openness to all people. Even when I'm going to people for the purpose of loving them and helping them, it all happens so fast. In visiting people in hospital, for instance, I dash all over town from one hospital to another. This doesn't sound very deep, nor as personal as it ought to be.

On one of my hospital days as I headed for the sick room of a patient, I walked near the nurses' station where an old lady was standing in her bathrobe. She wanted to go down to the lobby to buy a chocolate bar. No one would really listen to her, and it was obviously against the rules for any patient to venture off the floor. She felt frustrated and imprisoned. She just looked at me as I went walking by. Her eyes held me and made me stop. I listened to her as she began to talk to me. I couldn't help myself. I did what I almost never do. I took forty-five minutes out of what I thought was an important afternoon to sit with this seventy-four-year-old widow lady, of French and Jewish background and with the most beautiful gift of speech and thought, in spite of her trembling hands and body.

I sat entranced. She touched my heart. We became in just a few moments, dear friends. The nurses at the desk thought she was a bothersome old lady. But God said to me: "Arthur, you old fool: stop here. I have a beautiful angel who would speak to you."

I've been grateful ever since for those forty-five minutes. It was a magic time. It was Godspell. It was a blessing by the wayside.

That experience was a reminder. It said to me: Don't miss the call to be human when it comes. It may be a moment with the Divine. It may be a moment of immortality, of insight, of new faith, or of joy because you took a moment to love your neighbor and also found yourself loved, healed, and blessed.

It will be Jesus Himself out there on the journey of life who will be waiting by the roadside as someone in need, who needs each one of us.

LET'S DISCUSS

1. Do you agree with the author in his concept of who your "neighbor" is?

2. What are your own struggles with neighborliness?

3. What is different about Jesus' claim on us to "be a neighbor" from the generally accepted view of neighborliness?

4. Do you take time to stop and know people?

5. Is there anyone right now to whom, by your concern and caring, you are being a neighbor in Jesus' sense of the word?

6. Is the "cost" of being a neighbor worth it?

7. Have you ever taken "time you didn't have" to be a neighbor and found that God was in the experience?

8. Can a person learn to be a better neighbor than he is? Is there hope for us?

9. How does the cross fit into Jesus' call to Christians to be good neighbors?

10. If we went out looking for neighbors to love, would life be more exciting for us?

How to Love Your Enemy

Obviously, loving your enemy is the tough one. This is the one call of Christ that most defies our basic human instincts, such as our instinct to anger, our instinct to fight, and our moral and legal justification for the use of violence in the cause of self-defense.

We're supposed to love our parents. We're supposed to love our husbands, our wives, and our kids. We all know that. Even the secular society we live in gives us a bad time if we fail in those departments.

But our enemy! That asks from our souls a whole different spirit, an attitude so different from the world's attitude that we question if it can be held philosophically or lived practically at all.

It's because your enemy hates you. He envies you. He is prepared to destroy you—slowly and subtly, socially and spiritually, or suddenly, swiftly, violently, and viciously. And you have no defense, unless you change your enemy. And the risk in that is terrifying.

I knew someone who once took that risk. Consciously, deliberately, and with her eyes wide open, she dared to take it. She was a beautiful young woman and a creative artist. She lived on the west bank of our university campus neighborhood. Here she did her pottery, painting, sewing, and also her special artistry of helping other people.

But one soft, golden Sunday afternoon in the Minnesota autumn she went hitchhiking, wearing the leather suit and hat she had made and carrying the beautiful bag she had also made. She trusted the world and loved her brother-man. She believed that if she loved the world, the world would love her.

She was on her way to Des Moines to hear the Mason Proffits sing the songs she loved. Like:

> Walk on down the road, your hair blowin' free
> Take your time and remember what you want to be,
> We're all brothers and gotta learn how to live.
> Let's get together, 'cause we got a lot of love to give.

And she gave it so freely—believing literally what Jesus said. She did not know that there was an enemy waiting for her—that she would die that day by a country roadside far from home.

Her death raised all the questions about trust, about love, and about how you love the stranger in the world, the enemy waiting down the road. But later, tucked in the frame of her mirror, her parents found a scrap of paper with the words of Jesus written on it in her own hand, as a kind of credo:

> He gives His sunlight to both the evil and the good, and sends rain on the just and unjust, too. If you love only those who love you, what good is that? Even scoundrels do that much.

The price is so high. The risk is so great. The enemy is such a threat. So if you're a Christian, how do you love your enemy?

Jesus commands that you pray for him—because he is someone God loves. "There is a saying," Jesus reminds us, "Love your friends and hate your enemies. But I say, Love your enemies! Pray for those who persecute you. In that way," He says, "You will be acting as true sons of your Father in heaven. For He gives His sunlight to both the evil and the good, and sends rain on the just and the unjust, too."

You're probably not going to stand toe-to-toe with your enemy, glaring at him across the barrier of your differences, and just love him without any effort at all. There is no way that will happen, because if you really have an enemy—someone you're actually aware of as an enemy—there is a reason for not loving him. He has hurt you or you have hurt him. Something has come between you and built its own Berlin Wall or Iron Curtain. And something inside of you turns over and quivers when you even see that other person.

For most of us it isn't a matter of the known, willful enemy who is going to kill us. It's more likely to be someone we once loved, who was once our friend but who now is an enemy. Love turned sour, and two people began to see each other in a different way. They began to see the cracks in the character of the other, and began to concentrate on them, think about them, dwell on them, brood over them, and more and more to be offended and repulsed by them.

In the church I serve there was once a dear friend of mine, a man I loved and admired. I think he loved me. He thought I was great. But one day he said to me in his enthusiasm, "Arthur, you're our Jesus, our Messiah, in this town." And I just shuddered. I had a premonition at that moment that something had already gone wrong in our relationship, that this friend who was calling me Jesus now would be calling me the devil tomorrow. And that is exactly what has happened. The things I say and do and stand for only make him angry now. So, for years our relationship has been that of antagonists. We are enemies. And I still grieve for that lost friend.

It's so easy for the lover to become the hater and the friend to become the enemy. Even the husband or wife to become the bitter and deadly antagonists.

This means you're not likely to rise up and say to yourself, "Go to, I will now love my enemy. I mean, it's okay, whatever he did to me. I'll forget it. I'll just put it away. The slate is clean. Just like that." Now, we don't forget quite that easily. Jesus says it won't happen that way. He says "pray for those who persecute you." And then He says, "You will be acting as true sons of your Father in Heaven."

Isn't that because sons in the same family would accept the obligation to try harder with a brother—even to the point of trying to change a relationship that had palled and gone bad? It is because God loves your brother, your brother-man. He loves even the brother who becomes your enemy. He loves all His children. He does not hold back His blessing from any of them, even from the bad ones—the ones who have become someone's archenemy. That's what He's saying in the Bible: "For He gives His sunlight to both the evil and the good, and sends rain on the just and the unjust, too."

If God the Father can do good to His bad boys

and girls—letting His sun shine warm upon their days and His rain fall gently on their fields—and they're our brothers and sisters, who are we to withhold our love? Jesus says that the way for us to be like the Father in doing good to evil people and loving our enemy, is to pray for them.

It is prayer that changes the situation between you and your enemy. Prayer makes you look differently at your enemy. After all, your enemy looks like a sinister monster now. But when you pray for him, he is suddenly reduced to his simple humanity. You'll be able to see your enemy as a child of God.

And once we see our enemy in that different way, the whole relationship is actually changed. You are changed. But he, too, is changed. He can't help but be changed. Prayer releases power that does change people. And that power is love. The only way you ever get love or ever find it or ever recapture it when it's lost, is by prayer.

It's funny how different enemies can look after they've been prayed for and have become friends. It's funny how different the Japanese people look to us thirty years after Pearl Harbor. They looked so sinister and menacing in their role as Kamakazi pilots in their little Zero airplanes. We hated them! But now they're the beautiful people. We hated the Germans, but now Werner Von Braun is one of our space experts and Dr. Kissinger runs our foreign policy. Yet once the Germans were our enemies. I once had the delightful experience of performing the marriage of a young man whose father had been a German rocket scientist in World War II. His bride was a young woman whose father had been chairman of America's Civil Aeronautics Board during that same war. So love can change many things. And it is prayer that releases that power of love.

It's like the poem that says:

He drew a circle that shut me out —
Heretic, rebel, a thing to flout.
But love and I had the wit to win:
We drew a circle that took him in!

It is actually possible, Jesus says, if we pray for our enemy.

And that means for us to accept the challenge of love. "If you love only those who love you," Jesus says, "what good is that? Even scoundrels do that much. If you are friendly only with your friends, how are you different from anyone else? Even the heathen do that."

After all, we do make a big claim for ourselves as Christians. We say we're unique. We claim there's something different about us: that we're at least trying to live for different goals and by different values and through promoting a different kind of relationship among people.

We're suposed to be peculiar. The whole literature of Christianity underscores again and again that our business is to be oddballs. "Fools for Christ's sake," the Scripture says. Madmen for Jesus. Ready to do all kinds of strange, unsocial, non-country-club kinds of things—all for the sake of this unlettered country carpenter who lived in a little town with a bad reputation in the hill country of an insignificant nation two thousand years ago. It is madness, and we know it! But that's our "thing." It's what we're about! Remember what Peter said to his Christian friends: "You're not like the rest of the world. For you are 'a chosen generation, a royal priesthood, a holy nation, a peculiar people.' " He said, "You're to live a different, better life than anybody else. Because you're Jesus' people. It's part of the deal." Peter lays out the requirements of that high and exciting life: "Honor all men. Love the brotherhood. Fear God. Honor the king."

The ridiculous thing is that most of us somehow think that even after we are Christians we ought to be able to live just like everyone else. We think we ought to be just as free as the next guy to gossip, to put people down, to cut up the competition, to blow off steam, to give vent to our emotions, and to follow our basest human instincts—"because," we say, "we're human."

But Jesus says, "Hey, now. Don't give Me that. I never promised you a rose garden. I never told you it would be easy. I said that if you wanted to go My way and be My disciple you would have to count the cost first, and then deny yourself, and take up your cross and follow Me."

The Christian life is "the challenge of love. It is a call to be the "love people" in the world. We are to be the people who are committed to trying to do the loving thing, the thing that comes out of caring about others rather than the thing that puts our self-interest first.

But we too often do what the world says—that it's only "human" to put good old number one first. We do it in our families, we do it in our marriages, we do it on our street, in our town, and we even do it as a country! "America first, man, of course! My country, right or wrong!"

That's why Jesus is so radical. He threatens a lot of what we've let ourselves believe in and stand for.

We teach loving your neighbor, turning the other cheek, and that "thou shalt not kill." And yet we're horrified when an eighteen-year-old decides he is going to be a conscientious objector to war. We couldn't understand the hundreds of American young people who went to prison, left the country when that seemed to be their only way to refuse to bear arms.

We thunder ominously about "communists, socialists, hippies, and cowards," but we forget that it wasn't Karl Marx who got at them, but Jesus—good, old radical, earthshaking Jesus! Jesus is earthshaking and radical because He calls God's people to love, to fling themselves away for the world. He challenges them into doing everything in their power to reach out where others would run away, to touch in love where others would recoil in horror, to forgive where others would condemn and judge, to love an enemy and give him a chance to be a friend where others would let him remain an enemy forever.

It's so hard. But that is our calling, our duty, our obligation, and our crazy sort of life.

It's the sort of life that my friend Sandy, the beautiful hitchhiker, dared to live. People said of her after she died:

> She would go out of her way to help . . . she had utter confidence in everybody . . . she believed in love and peace.

A local columnist did an article on her, and he interviewed a Professor of Sociology at our university about why so many young girls today are not afraid to hitchhike. He said:

> The youth movement is based on love and peace and the idea is that trust will be recipro-

123

cated. There is a strong feeling of strangers sharing and coming to each other's assistance. The idea is that you love and get love back . . . that kind of romantic dream. It's respect for neighbor and trading kindness for kindness.

And then he observed:

Regretably, it doesn't always pay to express high ideas with strangers. It only takes one person to bring you down to earth or put you below it.

It's so very, very true in this evil world of enemies as well as friends. And that is exactly the challenge of love. Jesus accepted it, and appeared to have lost the cause. But did He? Actually He won something beautiful and infinite for all of us. And maybe that means that love, after all, really is absolute and deserves to be defended with our lives—to stand shoulder to shoulder with the One who was so willing to give His life.

Longfellow said:

The sole thing I hate is Hate;
For Hate is death; and Love is life,
And peace, a splendor from above;
And Hate, a never ending strife,
A smoke, a blackness from the abyss,
Where unclean serpents coil and hiss!
Love is the Holy Ghost within;
Hate is the unpardonable sin!
Who preaches otherwise than this
Betrays his Master with a kiss!

This is the challenge of love!

And this all asks of us so much. Inside we're beginning to feel: "You just can't expect that of ordinary mortals. Going that far for your enemy is too much!"

Yes, it is—especially if we insist on staying just the way we are, accepting our sin and our self-interest, making up our minds that this is the way it's going to be, and believing that we're simply going to live with it forever. But I don't think there are very many human beings who really do want to simply live with it. I don't think most of us like our sins. I think lots of us are unhappy with ourselves. We'd like so much to be better if we really thought we could be. Maybe that's why Jesus' challenge to us about loving our enemies is not to be ashamed to be perfect. "But you are to be perfect," He says, "even as your Father in Heaven is perfect."

We'd better get over the ideas that we're just sinners forever and that we haven't a chance and that God the Father and Christ our brother are on a different continuum from us or that they're magic like Captain Midnight and Superman and Buck Rogers all rolled into one and that they can do and be things we could never dream of doing and being.

Not so! "You will do the very works I do," Jesus said to His disciples, "and greater works will you do—if," He said, "*you believe.*" If you want to and if you care, all you have to do, Jesus said, is to ask: "Ask, and it will be given you." "You shall say to this mountain, remove hence to yonder place, and it will move!" We are meant to move mountains.

Maybe we are meant to be saints and not sinners. Maybe we were never intended to be satisfied with being sinners. Sure we love sinners. We forgive sinners and we accept them. But strive to *be* saints! "*Be ye perfect*" —just like God the Father. Wow!

And the biggest barrier to that, I'm convinced, is not our weak humanity, but rather our fear, our shame, and our suspicions that we won't be liked if we're too good. We might appear to have lost that tough cutting edge in the business world if we're too good. We won't be acceptable at the neighborhood coffees if we're too good.

And maybe we won't be. Maybe we will be the oddballs supreme, the superfreaks of all time. Maybe there won't be anyone who will want to have anything to do with us. But I doubt it. God, I think, will take care of that. He will make up for it. He'll show us new ways and new dimensions.

I breakfasted once with our state governor's legislative lieutenant, a beautiful Christian friend of mine. He told of his new life as a Christian, beginning the spring before, on Easter day in our church. He told about the change in his life. He cut out late drinking with the boys. He cut out the aggressive competitiveness against the opposition party. "I could feel myself falling out of favor in the inner circle of the governor's closest advisors," he said. "I could feel myself being bypassed in the most important decisions because of my new faith and new life-style." He continued, "It was a struggle. I was trying to be faithful—to purify my life, to have the spirit of love. But it hurt. Finally, I just said: 'God, I'm in Your hands. Maybe this will be the end, but I'm going to live the new life.' And then," he said, "to my surprise, when the time came that they needed someone for the most important job—of seeing the governor's legislative program through the legislature—suddenly Wendy (Governor Wendell Anderson of Minnesota) was calling me! Funny how God works things out."

Funny indeed, when we are faithful to our highest calling. When humbly and openly we dare to be better than we ever were. This means to love where we never loved before. This includes loving even our enemies.

It turns life around. It turns your enemy around. It makes him your friend. I think sometimes that I'm almost afraid to try. Maybe you have that feeling too. But Christians could pray for each other. And that might make us brave enough to try. That's when Jesus Christ might just bring us to the day when we can love all men with all our hearts—just as He does.

LET'S DISCUSS

1. *Do you think Jesus' claim on us to love our enemy is an impossibility?*

2. *Would you like to love your enemy, or do you secretly enjoy having him as an enemy?*

3. *Have you ever tried praying for people whom you felt were your enemies?*
   (a) Was it too hard to do?
   (b) Did it help at all?

4. *Was the girl who trusted the world wrong to do so, as the professor seemed to indicate? Should we all be more trusting?*

5. *If you love someone else first, does that help that other person to love you in return?*

6. *Is it realistic to think enemies can be changed?*
   (a) What about personal enemies?
   (b) What about international enemies?

7. *Is it fair to ask Christians to go beyond the law of "an eye for an eye" and to try to actually love those who have wronged them?*

8. *Does the higher law of love really work – if we give it a chance?*

9. Would you be willing to run the risk of loving everybody — even those who are bad, or who have a different philosophy from yours, or who have a different life-style?

10. How about being perfect? Is that worth a try even if we never succeed?

11

How to Love Yourself

Anyone who works with people knows that you have to love yourself. You have to believe in yourself. You have to think that you're somebody, that you have a right to live, and that it's okay to be alive.

Some of the deepest human tragedies any of us come across in life are those caused by, or somehow involving, people who hate themselves —people who think they are worthless, people with a low, low view of themselves.

People who hate themselves are dynamite. They strike out at other people and at the world. Because they despair of themselves, they cannot really care about others.

I think all of us have trouble loving ourselves. Most of us know very well what it's like to feel inferior. It's an effort to beef yourself up to feeling equal to some people you're going to be with. Take it from one who was called "Fatty" in grade school, and "Dumbo" on the basketball courts in ninth grade. There is no more awful hell, for a kid at least, than to feel in your bones that you are inferior.

All of us want to be accepted. There's not a soul among us who doesn't want to be admired; who doesn't want people to like him; and who doesn't want people to notice him and listen to what he has to say.

But people can sure cut you dead! Have you ever talked to someone and have the feeling that he doesn't even know you're there, that he's looking right through you? Two people confessed to me recently that they had had that experience right in the church. One girl said: "I kept saying 'hi' to other kids, and they didn't even answer me!" That doesn't make you feel as though you're somebody, does it?

How can we come to feel like somebody? How can we feel beautiful, wanted, intelligent, fulfilled, and happy? How can we feel we're among friends? How can we come to feel that our life, somehow, is special? How can we be assured that we're doing and being something that this world needs? In other words, how can we love ourselves?

I think the first thing God wants of us is to *see ourselves as His gift to the world*. That's a standard joke, of course: "Hey, hey gang! Look at me—God's gift to the world! God's gift to my company! God's gift to my high school. God's gift to my street, my town, my city!"

It's ridiculous, of course. It's something to laugh about. It sounds so boastful. It's just a big blowhard joke—a wiseacre big show.

And yet it is surprisingly true. Very deeply true. "It is by grace you are saved," Paul wrote to the Christians at Ephesus, "through trusting Him; it is not your own doing. It is God's gift. . . ."

We are something beautiful that God has done. We are something exquisite He has planned. And we'd better treat with appropriate awe and reverence the handiwork of God! We were created, designed, and custom-crafted by the Great Designer, especially for a particular time and place in His vast, complicated world. We each were hand-tooled and no product of any assembly line!

And we need to recover the wonder of that fantastic, beautiful process. We need to see ourselves as that unique creature God molded out of His mighty love and out of the mystery of His desires and designs too deep for human comprehension. Remember how James Weldon Johnson described it in his "God's Trombones:"

> . . .God said: I'm lonely still.
> Then God sat down —
> On the side of a hill where He could think:
> By a deep, wide river He sat down:
> With His head in His hands,
> God thought and thought,
> Till He thought: I'll make Me a man!
> Up from the bed of the river
> God scooped the clay;
> And by the bank of the river
> He kneeled Him down:
> And there the Great God Almighty
> Who lit the sun and fixed it in the sky,
> Who flung the stars to the most far corner
>   of the night,
> Who rounded the earth in the middle of His
>   hand:
> This Great God,
> Like a mammy bending over her baby,
> Kneeling down in the dust
> Toiling over a lump of clay
> Till He shaped it in His own image;
> Then into it He blew the breath of life,
> And man became a living soul.
> Amen. Amen.

You and me! A living soul, from the hand of God! Amen! We didn't make ourselves. We didn't force ourselves into the world. God wanted us. He still does want us. We're a gift. And we had nothing to do with it. We can't be blamed or praised. We are here by grace—sheer, undeserved, unmerited grace!

But if we're here and if we really come from the hand of God—then there has to be a reason. We may have lost sight of the reason. We may never have quite understood the reason. But no matter how we may have messed up, no matter what awful things we have done, and no matter what sins stain our record—we are what we are, good and bad, with our triumphs and tragedies, our good deeds and our bad habits, because God, bless His forgiving heart, is molding us, shaping us, and fashioning us, sometimes in the fire but always for His purposes.

It's like the little sparrows Jesus spoke of: "Are we not of greater value than they?" *We are of value.* We are a gift.

Very often we think we are disqualified. We think that because we know ourselves so well and hate so deeply those things within us with which we struggle. But listen, even the New Testament saints had those! Remember what Paul said? "That which I would I do not, and that which I would not, that I do. O wretched man that I am, who shall deliver me from this body of death?" And then he gives his great answer to his own question: "God alone, through Jesus Christ our Lord!—Thanks be to God!"

We may not very well understand this strange thing that we are. But we have a right, humbly and hopefully, to love it. I regret that as a Christian minister I do not yet know any better than I do the

Bible through and through. But I think God is doing something with this guy I call "me . . ." with this creaking back and graying hair and fuzzy eyes and faulty plumbing and rounded shoulders. Believe it or not, I'm even glad I've got my body and not someone else's! Even standing in the showers at the Sports and Health Club with all those young Greek gods and Charley Atlases standing around, I'm glad I'm me and mine.

Men "love their own bodies," Paul said. "No man ever hated his own body: on the contrary, he provides and cares for it, just as Christ treats the church, His body."

So it's okay. It's okay to be lovable—even to ourselves. We are God's gift to the world!

But God wants us even more than that to see ourselves as *creatures in Christ*—to see ourselves as people whose personalities are created by Christ, and formed and fashioned by our relationship with Christ.

Our life, Paul says to the Ephesians, "is not a reward for work done. There is nothing we can boast of, for we are God's handiwork, created in Christ Jesus. . . ."

Our problem isn't so much that we're boastful as it is that we are burdened. And they may be parts of the same problem! It's really a kind of arrogance to be weighed down with the impossible burden of our own lives. We are forever stacking the cards against ourselves: demanding of ourselves impossible deeds, and setting performance goals that are, as one of my young friends says, "out-a-state!"

We can't live the life we've given ourselves. We weren't meant to live this hurrying, hurtling ride into the unrealities of a success bought at the price of our sanity, of a profit simply paving the way for poverty of personality, and of a corporate recognition created for ourselves too often out of the cruel crushing of those we love most.

No wonder we hate ourselves! No wonder our communities are plagued with deep-seated feelings of guilt. Lots of us, claiming to be Christ's people, are denying Him in the very human relationships that are most sacred. We're living by double standards: building our professions on reputations of integrity and yet destroying personal God-given relationships by deception. A man wants to be known in his city as a top attorney, or a top accountant, or a leading corporation president—known for utter honesty in all his business dealings. He would be chagrined and ashamed if he were accused of being anything less than impeccable. But the fact that he is "cheating" on his wife—having an affair with another woman—and intends to leave his wife and children who need him, he puts in a whole separate compartment of his life. He tells himself that this activity in no way brings into question his integrity as a man, and therefore his whole honesty and trust as a professional is intact. But such a man is so naive. When he does it he's so blind! He thinks he's getting away with it. But you know what Jesus is saying to him? "Thou fool! This night thy soul shall be required of thee! For what does it profit a man if he gain the whole world, but lose his own soul!"

That is the kind of thing that happens when we leave life to ourselves. We are so ambitious! We allow ourselves to get so out-of-balance! We hurt so many people, including ourselves. And that demon down inside drives us, pushes us, and scourges us onward. And we are ridden with guilt.

And I want you to know I'm not writing this just about my fellow human beings. I do not condemn my brother Christians. We're in this life together. Satan has become one of the most powerful realities I know in suburbia. And I, too, am burdened! I, too, grab my life again and again, and run with it as though I were going to make the touchdown all by myself. It is as though I were going to save the world all by myself, as though I were going to win all the souls in town all by myself! So arrogant, so boastful, and so humanly proud—little me, the atlas of Edina or the colossus of Minneapolis holding up the world.

I'm ashamed of that. I've been there. I've heard the voice: "Thou fool, Arthur, thou fool."

I forget sometimes what Paul the apostle said, and what I should never have forgotten: "It is not I who live but Christ who liveth in me!" I am called to be a man in Christ. I was never meant to be a whole man, a complete person, without Christ. There's no future for any of us without Christ storming into our lives and toppling our ego from the throne and taking over the whole household of our heart. This is the only way! We've got to abandon ourselves to Christ.

He said it Himself: "The man who loves himself is lost, but he who hates himself in this world will be kept safe for eternal life. If anyone serves Me, he must follow Me." We have to love Christ in us. We have to love the Jesus who comes to take up residence in our souls. We then can begin to love what we find in ourselves. Then we will begin to find more and more the Spirit's gifts of "love, joy, peace, patience, kindness, goodness, fidelity, gentleness, and self-control."

These qualities are lovable. These are cause for gratitude. They make us glad for life. These make life worth living. Because "things" are in balance. Christ is the Lord. He is in charge and He reigns. And somehow He preserves us.

And you know how He does that? Oftentimes Christ preserves us by others who care. Unknown others. One day I talked on the phone with a minister I had never met. And yet many mutual friends had said, "You two have got to meet." One of my people said: "You two are like peas in a pod. You ought to know each other."

So finally we were on the phone, and he said: "We've never met, Arthur, but I have heard of your work, and I know of you." And then he said, "I have been praying for you for three years." We'd never even met, and he was praying for me as a brother.

That minister out there cared about me. And so many of my Christian friends cared about me. And that caring helped me to get back to center, as a man created in Christ. A man with Christ at the top. Living for Christ!

It's the only way.

A young minister friend who was dying had the same experience. He was given a new intern over at the county hospital where he was battling leukemia. "You've never met me," this young man said, "but I know you. I've been praying for you for months."

Our lives must have a purpose. We have to be going somewhere, living for something, and heading out toward a goal. And there's only one goal for the Christian. There's only one thing worth doing if Jesus is Lord of our lives, and we serve the King with honor. *And that's doing good.* We're here to do good in the world. Christ dwells in our hearts to give us power to do good. Every Christian knows that he is no good unless he is doing some kind of good. Loving yourself is ultimately a product of knowing in your heart that you're doing somebody some good: to some other human being or to some group of human beings. The ultimate despair is to feel you are no longer useful—that you're no good to anybody. And, really, there isn't anybody in this world who is no good to nobody. Everyone is some good to somebody—if he lets Christ into his heart, and lets Him take over and lead.

Here it is in the Bible: the final prescription for loving ourselves. Paul says, "For we are . . . created in Christ Jesus to devote ourselves to the good deeds for which God has designed us."

We may have thought that the next promotion in the company or that terrific job in New York or that second snowmobile or that power boat or trading in your wife for that beautiful other woman or that idyllic life of ease after retirement was going to be the answer to happiness, peace, fulfillment, and satisfaction with ourselves. But it never is. Never.

Our real happiness, our real peace with ourselves, comes with doing the good for which God designed us. That's what makes us really happy: when we're "on track," "in tune," and "in the Spirit" with God's whole plan and purpose for our lives.

The hymns tell us that Christ was born to die. It was His inevitable purpose, which leads me to say, find what you were born for, friend. In fact, Christian friends can help each other find together what each of them was born for. I trust my Christian brothers to help me find what I was born for because I don't always know. I think it's to preach and preach and preach. But sometimes I feel so tired, and I think there must be something else. But then, in the end, at a hospital bedside, holding the hand of a lonely and frightened friend, or fighting in prayer for the life of someone who's desperate and dying—there I'm alive. There I feel the power on the Lord. There I'm happy. There I like being me. And it's all worthwhile.

In the long sweep of things, after considering the Saint Pauls and the Francis of Assisis and the John Wesleys and the Father Damiens and the Albert Schweitzers and the Elizabeth Saints and the Martin Luther Kings and the Jim Turpins—we feel terribly traditional and awfully middle-class and, in a sense, far removed from Galilee and its gallant hero who walked in the sun, who made men one, and who finally suffered on a cross before men saw that He was God among them.

But maybe Jerusalem or New York or Memphis or Dallas is not where all of us were meant to be. Maybe our own street or our office building or our sales territory is where some of us are meant to be. Maybe, loving the world that is there in your life is the most exciting, fulfilling, satisfying thing you could possibly do with our life.

In a beautiful book about the Quakers and the growth of their movement in loving service at great personal sacrifice, there is a tender word on witness from the diary of Ann Traylor, the English servant girl who went to the new world with her mission and was raped on shipboard. She tells of being with Henrietta Best when she died—both of them in an American prison for their faith. Henrietta Best had herself been raped decades before in France by soldiers of the Cardinal. Ann Traylor wrote in her diary from prison:

> But one thing is irrefutable: the death of her children and her rape by the soldiers of the Cardinal were given some sense when I collapsed in her arms in the hold of the ship and breathed to her in horror that I had been raped. She could say to me, "Hush, it happened to me, too." And those words saved my life and my reason. What resurrected me, were her love and her understanding, which, clearly, were the fruit of her own suffering; she could identify with me without pious pretense. When she consoled me and took me in her arms, I experienced the presence of God. So I found out that, indeed, God needs us as much as we need Him. For it is only in our acts that He can fully express Himself. In one thing, Margaret Fell was incontestably right: miracles are immaterial. Man, in his ultimate despair, is not helped by an omnipotence who, like a magician in a cosmic circus, suspends the laws of nature. If God is anything at all, He is what St. John said He was, what George Fox said He was and what Margaret Fell, bless her soul, showed He was: LOVE. All other definitions are efforts on our part to evade the demands of that final realization.

You could die in a prison holding a fellow sufferer to your heart, and be glad you were you. After all the angers, guilt, doubt, loneliness, and pain, you could love yourself because you were doing a good thing—a very small good deed—for God.

With Christ in our heart, knowing that we, even we, are God's unique gift to the world, we could do it. With a big smile of *joy*, we could do it. We could help each other. I love you, friends. I am feeling for you, just as you are with all your needs. I am with you. And Jesus Christ is with us all.

Thank God for that.

LET'S DISCUSS

1. Is there anything you would honestly have to say you do not like about yourself – some habit, some feeling, some desire, or some memory?

2. Has it been hard for you to believe that God loves you even with those secret faults?

3. Have you ever had an "inferiority complex"? Do you still have it?

4. If any of the above are true, how are you going to live with yourself for the rest of your life? Don't you think God wants something better than self-recrimination and guilt for you?

5. Have you ever thought of yourself as God's gift to the world? Does that idea help?

6. If Christ is in you, doesn't it make sense that you are of unique and special value?

7. In what ways have you put intolerable demands and burdens on yourself?

8. If we don't manage our lives very well by living for ourselves and for our own ambitions, is there any reason to think we might do better if we were to live for Christ – with Him in charge of our lives?

9. How about "doing good" as a goal? Would that be a big enough goal for your life?

10. Might you love yourself a little more if you should discover that your goal of doing some good for somebody was actually being fulfilled?